Messedesign
Jahrbuch 2003/2004

Trade Fair Design
Annual 2003/2004

Karin Schulte

Messedesign
Jahrbuch 2003/2004

Trade Fair Design
Annual 2003/2004

avedition

Inhaltsverzeichnis
Contents

„... aber das heißt nicht, daß ich alle diese Bücher im Bordone-Saal ausgelesen hätte, ich habe niemals in meinem Leben ein einziges Buch ausgelesen, meine Art zu lesen ist die eines hochgradig talentierten Umblätterers, also eines Mannes, der lieber umblättert, als liest, der also Dutzende, unter Umständen Hunderte von Seiten umblättert, bevor er eine einzige liest ..."

Thomas Bernhard in:
Alte Meister, Frankfurt am Main 1988

"...but that doesn't mean that I had read all those books in the Bordone room. I have never in my entire life finished reading a single book. When it comes to reading, I am extremely talented in leafing through books, that is to say that I am a man who prefers to leaf through rather than to read, who will leaf through dozens if not hundreds of pages before reading a single one…"

Thomas Bernhard in:
Old Masters (Alte Meister), Frankfurt am Main 1988

Einleitung
Introduction

Nach Definition des § 64 Abs. 1 GewO ist eine Messe „eine zeitlich begrenzte im allgemeinen regelmäßig wiederkehrende Veranstaltung, auf der eine Vielzahl von Ausstellern das wesentliche Angebot eines oder mehrerer Wirtschaftszweige ausstellt und überwiegend nach Muster an gewerbliche Wiederverkäufer, gewerbliche Verbraucher oder Großabnehmer vertreibt."

Die in diesem Buch gesammelte Auswahl berücksichtigt 58 Messeauftritte zwischen Januar 2002 und Ende März 2003 im deutschsprachigen Raum, die in chronologischer Reihenfolge aufgenommen wurden. Es sind nur Messestände, die zu oben angegebener Definition passen, absichtlich wurden keine Ausstellungen und keine Expos einbezogen. Ich bin der Meinung, dass dort andere Maßstäbe angesetzt werden müssen und dies eine eigene Publikation erfordern würde.

Die Auswahl ist eine persönliche, subjektive Auswahl. Kriterien für die Aufnahme sind insbesondere die übergeordnete Entwurfsidee und gestalterische Qualität, aber auch das infrastrukturelle Funktionieren, die Präsentation der Exponate (sofern es überhaupt „Exponate" gibt), die für den Messestand verwendeten Materialien, die Beleuchtung, das Farbkonzept, die Grafik und die Einbindung von Events. Auch wenn das Budget inzwischen bei fast allen Firmen deutlich kleiner ist, entstehen immer wieder verblüffende, spannende Messeauftritte, die mittlerweile gestalterisch sehr anspruchsvoll sind. Dies gilt für einen großen Teil von Ständen nach wie vor nicht. Gut gestaltete Messestände sind nicht die Regel, sondern die Ausnahme.

Der Messestand soll Begegnungs- und Erlebnisraum sein, um die Position einer Marke langfristig im Kopf des Käufers zu verankern. Die offene Produktpräsentation, d.h. das bloße Ausstellen, kann dabei auch in den Hintergrund treten. Marketingexperten verstehen den Messestand als Kommunikationsplattform für Prozesse, Strategien und Haltungen. Ein gutes Messekonzept ist in das Marketingkonzept sowie die Vernetzung mit der Corporate Identity und dem Corporate Design des Unternehmens eingebunden (vgl. die Ausschreibungsunterlagen des ADAM 2002).

According to § 64 Section 1 of the Trade Act (Gewerbeordnung), a trade fair is "a generally regularly recurring event of a limited duration, at which a multitude of exhibitors exhibit the essential goods or services of one or more branch of industry and predominantly sell to commercial retailers, commercial consumers or bulk purchasers."

The selection compiled for this book takes account of 58 trade fair appearances between January 2002 and the end of March 2003 in the German-speaking countries, which are included in chronological order. Only those trade fairs fitting the aforementioned definition were considered; exhibitions and expos were excluded intentionally. In my opinion other standards have to be adopted for the latter, which would necessitate a publication of their own.

The selection is a personal, subjective one. The criteria for inclusion are, above all, the overriding design idea and design quality, but also the functional quality of the infrastructure, the presentation of the exhibits (in as far as there are any "exhibits"), the materials used for the trade fair stand, the lighting, the colour concept, the graphics and the integration of events. Even though in the meantime the budget of most companies is significantly smaller, time and again we witness amazing, exciting trade fair appearances of a very high design quality. This still does not apply for the majority of stands, though. Well-designed trade fair stands remain the exception rather than the rule.

The trade fair stand should be a place to meet and enjoy experiences, to fix a brand's position in the heads of the buyers. The open product presentation, i.e. the actual exhibiting, can also fade into the background; the product itself does not have to be at the forefront. Marketing experts see the trade fair as a communication platform for processes, strategies and positions. A good trade fair concept is tied up with the marketing concept as well as the Corporate Identity and Corporate Design of a company (cf. the invitation of tenders for ADAM 2000).

Der Messeauftritt ist für das Unternehmen ein zentrales Element in der direkten Kommunikation, mit dem Ziel der Pflege bereits funktionierender Geschäftsbeziehungen oder Kontakte und der Akquisition (potentieller) neuer Kunden. Die Ziele (Aufmerksamkeit erzeugen, sich vom Umfeld abheben, den Dialog anregen, den Besucher mit einem unvergesslichen Erlebnis für sich gewinnen und binden) sind alt, aber die Methoden verändern sich.

Der Messeauftritt einer Firma ist heute nicht nur Ausstellung, sondern emotionale Erlebniswelt (Jahrmarkt, Theater, Show und Event), bei der viele organisatorische, gestalterische und dramaturgische Einflüsse zusammenkommen. Er muss Aufmerksamkeit erregen und sich deswegen deutlich von der benachbarten Konkurrenz unterscheiden. Er muss hervorstechen aus der Masse der Botschaften. Der Besuch muss so angenehm gestaltet sein, dass der Besucher weniger Zeit am Stand der Konkurrenz verbringt und sich lange wohl fühlt.

Das Interesse des Besuchers an einem Produkt oder einer Dienstleistung kann nicht nur mit Hilfe der Architektur geweckt werden: das sinnliche und emotionale Angesprochensein entsteht durch Bild, Licht, Ton, neue Präsentationstechniken und Marketing-Events, die früher nur als Entertainment auf integrierten Bühnen stattfanden und heute Bestandteil des gesamten Standkonzepts sind. Die Disziplinen Messeauftritt und Event wachsen zusammen, wobei der Event die Marke subtil unterstützen soll und sich sinnvoll ins Standkonzept einfügen muss.

Es geht um mehr als die Summe von Standarchitektur und Show, heute ist eine intelligente Form von Infotainment gefragt. In Zeiten von städtischen Themenparks, Einkaufs-Erlebniswelten (Showrooms wie Messeauftritte, Flagshipstores), inszenierten Jubiläumsgalas oder sonstigen Firmenveranstaltungen, Kongressen, inszenierten Markeneinführungen im städtischen Kontext (z.B. die Einführung der Mercedes-Benz A-Klasse mit der „A-Motion Tour") und Markendauerinszenierungen als Ereignis (z.B. die VW-Autostadt) muss auch der Besucher der Messe über die ganzheitliche Inszenierung von Markenerlebnis-

For a company, the trade fair appearance is a central element in direct communication, with the aim of cultivating existing functioning business relations or contacting and acquiring (potential) new clients. The aims (drawing attention, standing out from the surroundings, provoking dialogue, winning over and creating a bond with the visitor through an unforgettable experience) are old, but the methods change.

Today, a company's trade fair appearance is not only an exhibition, but also an emotional world of experiences (funfair, theatre, show and event) in which many organisational, structural and dramatic influences come together. It has to attract attention and for this reason it has to differ significantly from the neighbouring competitors. It has to stand out from the masses. The visit should be so pleasantly arranged that the visitor spends less time on the competitors' stands and feels at ease for a long while.

The visitor's interest in a product or service cannot be awakened with the help of architecture alone: addressing the senses and emotions is achieved through images, light, sound, new presentation techniques and marketing events that previously only took place as entertainment on integrated stages and today are an integral part of the complete trade fair concept. The disciplines trade fair appearance and event are fusing, whereby the event should subtly back the brand and has to fit meaningfully into the trade fair concept.

It is more than a question of the sum of the stand architecture and show; today an intelligent form of infotainment is called for. In these times of urban theme parks, shopping theme worlds (showrooms as well as trade fair appearances, flagship stores), staged anniversary galas or other such company events, congresses, staged brand introductions in an urban context (e.g. the introduction of the Mercedes-Benz A-Class with the "A-Motion Tour") and fixed events to promote a brand (e.g. the VW Car City), the trade fair visitor has to be reached by the integral staging of brand experiences. The marketing event has to be a balancing act of entertainment/enthusiasm on the part

sen erreicht werden. Der Marketing-Event muss ein Spagat von Unterhaltung/Begeisterung des Publikums und Informationsvermittlung sein, ein komplexes Zusammenspiel unterschiedlicher Gestaltungsinstrumente.

Würde man versuchen, verschiedene Eventtypen in diesem Buch zu unterscheiden, könnte man differenzieren zwischen:
– dem Messestand selbst als Event, der zu erlebnisorientierter Kommunikation führt (z.B. die diesjährige Präsentation der D'Art Design Gruppe auf der Euroshop in Düsseldorf)
– dem Einsatz von Prominenten, unabhängig von den Inhalten der Produkte oder Dienstleistungen des Ausstellers (z.B. im Jahr 2002 bei Tenovis auf der CeBIT)
– der Infotainment-Show auf der Event-Bühne, die versucht, mit einem Moderator die Verbindung von Information und Entertainment zu bewerkstelligen (z.B. im Jahr 2002 die moderierte Produktpräsentation bei Giesecke & Devrient auf der CeBIT.)
– dem Informationsparcours, bei dem der Besucher selbst aktiv wird (z.B. beim Parcours zur Ausstellung „Constructing Atmospheres" auf der light + building 2002)
– den abgeschirmten Erlebnisräumen, die Erholung vom Messetrubel bieten, ausgestattet mit „Lounge-Möbeln", „Chill-out-Music" und Cocktailbar (z.B. bei O$_2$ auf der CeBIT 2003 oder bei Denz auf dem Designers' Saturday 2002)
– der Einbeziehung von Kunst und Kultur (Nicht nur innerhalb der Messe spielen Events eine immer wichtigere Rolle. Zu einigen Messen gibt es mittlerweile Kulturprogramme, die die Messe in die Stadt tragen, etwa zur Kölner Internationalen Möbelmesse, zur light + building in Frankfurt.)
Fazit: Raum, Kommunikation und Event werden in Zukunft immer stärker miteinander verschmelzen.

Karin Schulte
Stuttgart, September 2003

of the public and the conveying of information, a complex interaction of different design instruments.

If one was to attempt to differentiate types of events in this book, one could distinguish between:
– The trade fair stand itself as an event leading to experience-orientated communication (e.g. this year's presentation by the D'Art Design Group at the Euroshop in Duesseldorf).
– The employment of VIPs, independent of the content of the exhibitor's products or services (e.g. Tenovis in 2002 at the CeBIT).
– The infotainment show on the event stage, which attempts to make a connection between information and entertainment using a presenter (e.g. in 2002 the product presentation at Giesecke & Devrient at the CeBIT).
– The information course where the visitors themselves become active (e.g. on the course belonging to the "Constructing Atmospheres" exhibition at the Light + Building 2002).
– The screened-off theme areas that offer visitors the chance to recover from the hurly-burly of the trade fair, equipped with "lounge furniture", "chill-out music" and cocktail bar (e.g. O$_2$ at the CeBIT 2003 or Denz at the Designers' Saturday 2002).
– The inclusion of art and culture. (Events do not only play an increasingly larger role within the trade fair. Several trade fairs in the meantime offer cultural programmes that take the trade fair into town, for example the Cologne International Furniture Fair and the Light + Building in Frankfurt.)
On balance: Communication and events will merge even more in the future.

Karin Schulte
Stuttgart, September 2003

Bänderspiel

Strip Show

thutundknup
für Création Baumann

thutundknup
for Création Baumann

Der frei stehende Stand ist von einem textilen Bändervorhang verhüllt. Schon von Ferne sieht man die fast 6 m hohen, schmalen, leicht wehenden Textilstreifen, die beim Näherkommen sich wandelnde Einblicke ermöglichen. Will man den Stand betreten, muss man sich wie durch Türvorhänge seinen Weg bahnen.

Im Innern sind entlang einer Mittelachse raumhohe Einzelstoffbahnen aufgehängt; und wie schon in den Vorjahren werden die verschiedenartigen Stoffgruppen vor hinterleuchteten Winkelelementen präsentiert. Die Servicemodule trennen den Ausmusterungs- vom Barbereich.

A curtain of textile strips envelops the freestanding trade fair stand. The almost 6-metre-high, narrow, gently swaying textile strips are visible from a distance and, upon approaching the stand, permit changing views of the interior. To enter the stand, one is forced to fight one's way through, as though through a curtained doorway.

Ceiling-high individual lengths of fabric are hung up in the interior along a centre line and, as in previous years, the varying fabric groups are presented in front of backlit angular elements. The service modules divide the display area from the bar area.

Year	**2002**
Location	**Frankfurt a. M.**
Trade Fair	**Heimtextil**
Exhibitor	**Création Baumann, Langenthal (CH)**
Architect	**thutundknup, Zurich (CH):** **Peter Knup, Benjamin Thut**
Lighting	**Showtech, Steffisburg (CH)**
Size	**300 m²**
Realisation	**Dietrich Display GmbH, Friolzheim**
Graphics / Communication	**thutundknup, Zurich (CH)**
Photos	**thutundknup, Zurich (CH)**

Aufgehängt
Hung Up

häfelinger + wagner design
für rohi Stoffe

häfelinger + wagner design
for rohi Stoffe

Der kleine Stand, der Teil der Neugestaltung des gesamten Unternehmenserscheinungsbildes ist, wird durch eine zentrale Wandscheibe in zwei Bereiche geteilt. Der eine Bereich mit der zentralen Rückwand als Präsentationsfläche dient dem Verkaufsgespräch. Die farbigen Stoffe, die an einfachen Haken mit großen Ösen aufgehängt sind, können schnell präsentiert werden und bilden zudem noch ein gestaltendes Wandmuster.

Der zweite Bereich dient dem ungezwungenen Besprechen und der Entspannung. Schlichte kubische Kissenelemente sind mit rohi-Stoffen bezogen, greifen so das farbige Spiel der aufgehängten Stoffe wieder auf und zeigen sie in realer Anwendung.

The small stand, which is part of the new design of the overall corporate appearance, is divided into two areas by a central wall panel. Sales talks are held in one of the areas, which has the central rear wall as a presentation surface. The colourful fabrics with large eyelets, which are hung up on simple hooks, are able to be presented quickly and, in addition, form a developing wall pattern.

The second area is used for informal meetings and relaxing. Simple cubic cushion elements are covered with rohi fabrics and thereby take up again the colourful display of the hung-up fabrics by showing them put to real use.

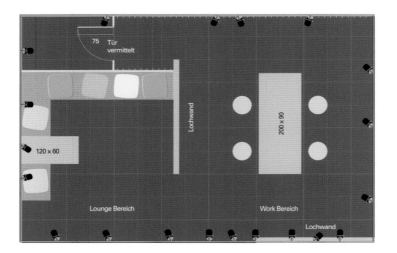

Grundriss

Plan

Year	**2002**
Location	**Frankfurt a. M.**
Trade Fair	**Heimtextil**
Exhibitor	**rohi stoffe GmbH, Geretsried**
Architect	**häfelinger + wagner design, Munich: Thomas Häussler, Frank Wagner**
Lighting	**dergrünefisch, Munich: Elke Gutjahr**
Size	**37.5 m²**
Realisation	**dergrünefisch, Munich: Elke Gutjahr Schreinerei Jacoby, Starnberg**
Graphics / Communication	**häfelinger + wagner design, Munich**
Photos	**Michael Heinrich, Munich**

Vorhangfall
Curtained Affair

Matteo Thun
für Vorwerk

Matteo Thun
for Vorwerk

Helle Vorhänge, die von hoch oben herunterfallen, machen den sehr großzügigen Messestand in seiner ganzen Höhe wahrnehmbar und erinnern an Installationen von Lilly Reich aus den 20er-Jahren des vorigen Jahrhunderts („Café Samt und Seide") oder die Schweiz-Präsentation auf der Frankfurter Buchmesse 1998.

Innerhalb dieses fast symmetrischen und streng strukturierten Raumes entwickelt sich auf einem hellen Teppichboden eine fast wohnliche Interieurszene, die durch ihre eigenständige Raumphilosophie und hohe Gestaltungsqualität überzeugt und zum Verweilen einlädt.

Pale curtains, draped from a great height, give this very spacious stand in its full height its striking appearance and are reminiscent of Lilly Reich installations from the 1920s (the Velvet and Silk Café) or of Switzerland's presentation at the 1988 Frankfurt Book Fair.

An almost homely interior scene has been created on a pale carpet within this virtually symmetrical and strictly structured area; it is both convincing in its individual spatial philosophy and high design quality as well as cosily inviting.

Möbel aus amerikanischem Nussbaum mit mattem Finish und Edelstahlprofilen unterstreichen die Wohnzimmeratmosphäre: eine überlange Anrichte zur Präsentation der Mustermappen mit doppelseitigen Stehpultaufsätzen, auf denen man je ein Buch aufschlagen kann sowie im offenen Besprechungsbereich flache Tische, belegt mit unterschiedlichen Teppichböden zu niedrigen Sitzbänken.

American walnut furniture with a matte finish and stainless-steel profiles enhances the living room atmosphere: an unusually long sideboard for presenting the books of samples with double-sided high lecterns, each able to hold one opened book, in addition to flat tables, covered with various carpets, and low benches in the open conference area.

Der Besprechungs-
und Bewirtungsbereich
in seiner ebenfalls
strengen Symmetrie
„verschwindet" hinter
der textilen Rückwand.

The meeting and
catering area, with its
equally strict symmetry,
"disappears" behind
the textile rear wall.

Year	**2002**
Location	**Frankfurt a. M.**
Trade Fair	**Heimtextil**
Exhibitor	**Vorwerk & Co. Teppichwerke GmbH & Co. KG, Hameln**
Architect	**Matteo Thun, Milan (I)**
Size	**350 m²**
Realisation	**Bluepool AG, poolgroup Zeissig, Springe-Völksen**
Photos	**G. Rupprath, Frankfurt a. M.**

Fliegende Teppiche
Flying Carpets

Christian Werner Industrial Design
für Carpet Concept

Christian Werner Industrial Design
for Carpet Concept

Innerhalb einer Rahmenstruktur aus weißen Stützen und Traversen fließen wellenförmig weinrot leuchtende Teppichbahnen vom Boden über die Wände und die Decke wieder zum Boden. Sie flankieren die an den beiden Längsseiten gegenüberliegenden Eingänge in den Stand. Ein Teil der Produktpräsentation wird zu einem Bestandteil der Architektur des Messestandes und vor allem zu einem einprägsamen Bild.

Innerhalb dieser von den fliegenden Teppichbahnen überdachten Fläche dient eine umlaufende schwarze Bank mit ihrer Rückenlehne nach außen hin als zusätzliche Abgrenzung, innen bildet sie außerdem Ablage und Bord für Musterbücher. Ein dezenter orientalischer Klangteppich unterstützt Erinnerungen an die Herkunft der Inszenierung.

Within a structural frame of white supports and cross-beams, bright bordeaux-coloured lengths of carpet flow in a wavelike fashion from the floor over the walls and ceiling and back down to the floor. In this way they flank the two entrances to the stand on the opposite-facing long sides. Part of the product presentation is thus turned into an integral part of the architecture of the trade fair stand and, above all, into an arresting image.

Serving as an additional boundary is a black bench, its backrest facing outwards, that skirts the inside of this area covered over by flying lengths of carpet. On the inside is storage space and shelving for books of samples. A subtle blanket of oriental sounds helps to conjure up associations with the origins of the setting.

CARPET
CONCEPT

Wie neugierige
Schlangen winden sich
die Teppichbahnen
aus dem Grundgerüst
und treiben ein Spiel
mit Farbe und Form.

The lengths of carpets
wind their way out
of the skeletal structure
like curious snakes,
playing games with
colour and form.

Year	**2002**
Location	**Hanover**
Trade Fair	**Domotex**
Exhibitor	**Carpet Concept Objekt-Teppichboden GmbH, Bielefeld**
Architect	**Christian Werner Industrial Design, Hollenstedt / Appel: Christian Werner, Ernst Kopold**
Lighting	**Kreon**
Size	**80 m²**
Realisation	**Viva Messebau, Hanover Tischlerei Oliver Cosmann, Hamburg**
Photos	**Soenne, Aachen**

Rahmenspiel

Framed

thutundknup
für Forum 8

thutundknup
for Forum 8

Das Forum 8 ist eine Aussteller- und Interessengemeinschaft von acht kreativen Schweizer Fabrikanten für Möbel und Licht. Der Ausstellungsraum auf der Messe in Köln ist in acht gleich große Streifen geteilt. Sie sind unter einem weißen, textilen Dach zusammengefasst, das die Sicht auf die Hallenarchitektur einschränkt.

Der rechteckige Raum wird über einen Mittelgang erschlossen. Quer zu diesem sind die einzelnen Kompartimente der jeweiligen Firmen mit Tüchern, die an einem Baustellengerüst verspannt sind, voneinander getrennt. Jedem dieser Bereiche ist eine eigene Farbe zugewiesen, die sich vom Boden über die Seitenwände zieht und so einen eigenen Farbraum schafft. Die dort präsentierten Produkte werden von engen Lichtkegeln angestrahlt.

Forum 8 is an interest group for exhibitors formed by eight creative Swiss furniture and light manufacturers. The exhibition area at the Cologne trade fair is divided into eight equal strips. These are brought together beneath a white textile roof that restricts the view of the hall's architecture.

The rectangular area is accessed by a central passageway. The individual compartments of each company are positioned at right-angles to the passageway and are separated by pieces of cloth that are stretched across scaffolding. A different colour has been assigned to each of these areas; the colour is carried from the floor over the side walls, thereby creating an independent coloured space. Narrow beams of light illuminate the products that are presented here.

Faszinierend ist ein kleiner Eingriff, der eine optische Täuschung erzeugt: die Tücher, die die Bereiche trennen, haben auf Augenhöhe einen horizontal liegenden Ausschnitt. Dieser wird vom ersten Rahmen, wenn man den Raum betritt, bis zum letzten, der die Bar am Ende des Standes abgrenzt, immer kleiner, so dass sich eine perspektivische Wirkung ergibt.

One small fascinating feature creates an optical illusion: the pieces of cloth separating the areas have a horizontal opening cut out at eye level. These become progressively smaller – from the first frame at the entrance to the area to the last frame verging on the bar at the end of the stand – and thereby create a sense of perspective.

Year	**2002**
Location	**Cologne**
Trade Fair	**International Furniture Fair**
Exhibitor	**Forum 8**
Architect	**thutundknup, Zurich (CH): Peter Knup, Benjamin Thut**
Lighting	**Showtech, Steffisburg (CH)**
Size	**634 m²**
Realisation	**Dietrich Display GmbH, Friolzheim**
Graphics / Communication	**thutundknup, Zurich (CH)**
Photos	**thutundknup, Zurich (CH)**

Blaue Glasbox
Blue Glass Box

Leitner GmbH
für ICF

Leitner GmbH
for ICF

Beim Messeauftritt eines italienischen Automobilkonzerns auf das Standsystem Leitner_10 aufmerksam geworden, entschied sich ICF spa aus Mailand für einen ebenerdigen Stand aus diesem System. Der Firmenphilosophie, zeitloses Design mit langlebigen Materialien und herausragendem Service zu verbinden, wird mit diesem hochwertigen System Rechnung getragen.

Es entstand ein leuchtender, transparenter Stand mit einem großzügigen Präsentationsbereich für die showroomartige Ausstellung der Produkte, die wie Ausstellungsobjekte punktuell ausgeleuchtet sind und sich so von der ebenmäßigen Beleuchtung des Standinneren absetzen. In fünf unterschiedlich inszenierten, aber durchaus authentischen Raumsituationen konnten mögliche Alternativen für die Gestaltung von Arbeitsplätzen oder Konferenz- und Besprechungsbereichen gezeigt werden.

After their attention had been drawn to the Leitner_10 stand system of an Italian automobile group at an automobile exhibition, ICF SpA of Milan opted for a ground-level system stand from this system. This high-quality system pays tribute to the company's philosophy of combining timeless design with durable materials and impeccable service.

A brightly-lit, transparent stand was created with a generous showroom-like presentation area for exhibiting the products. These products are illuminated with spotlights, like exhibits, and consequently stand out from the evenly lit interior of the stand. Possible alternatives for the design of workplaces or conference and meeting areas were able to be shown in five differently stage-managed but perfectly authentic spatial situations.

Die blauen, bis zu fast 30 m langen und 4,5 m hohen Glaswände des form- und farbreduzierten Kubus sind mit Schrift beklebt, die Rückwandseite ist geschlossen und beherbergt Lagerräume und Küche.

The cube, with its reduced form and colour, has blue glass walls almost 30m long and 4.5m high with adhesive lettering. The rear-wall side is closed and houses the storage rooms and kitchen.

Produktpräsentation
auf einem 12 m lan-
gen, von unten be-
leuchteten Podest und
an einem überlangen
Konferenztisch in
einem stützenfreien
Raum.

Product presentation
on a 12-metre-long
platform, lit from
below, and on an
excessively long con-
ference table in a
support-free area.

Year	**2002**
Location	**Cologne**
Trade Fair	**International Furniture Fair**
Exhibitor	**ICF spa, Vignate / Milan (I)**
Architect	**ICF spa, Vignate / Milan (I): Mr. Consuelo Cordini Leitner GmbH, Waiblingen: Alexander Recher**
Lighting	**Leitner GmbH, Waiblingen with: Fa. Sill**
Size	**342 m²**
Realisation	**Leitner GmbH, Waiblingen: Leitner Services GmbH**
Graphics / Communication	**ICF spa, Vignate / Milan (I)**
Photos	**Frank Erber, Ostfildern**

NILS HOLGER MOORMANN
NILS HOLGER MOORMANN
NILS HOLGER MOORMANN

Stoffkubus
Fabric Cube

Moormann Möbel GmbH
Eigenstand

Moormann Möbel GmbH,
Own Stand

Wie in jedem Jahr ist der Stand von Moormann Möbel ein Beispiel, wie man mit geringem Budget einen eindrucksvollen Messestand entwickeln kann. Die Außenwände des sehr geschlossen wirkenden Standes werden mit einem der Produkte aus der Kollektion von Moormann Möbel gebildet: dem Regalsystem „Egal", das gleichzeitig auch ausgestelltes Möbel ist. Nach außen schließen schwere rostrote Stoffbahnen, die wie Umzugsdecken wirken, den zeltartigen Raum ab. Der Firmenname ist – wie bei manchem Designer-Kleidungsstück – auf kleinen Etiketten, die an diese Stoffe angenäht sind, zu lesen.

As is the case every year, Moormann Möbel's stand is an example of how an impressive trade fair stand can be developed on a low budget. The external walls of the stand, which has a very closed appearance, are formed with one of the products from the Moormann Möbel collection: the "Egal" shelve system, which is at the same time a furniture exhibit. Rust-coloured lengths of fabric, which have the appearance of removal blankets, form the external border of the tent-like area. The company name is to be seen on small labels sewn on to these fabrics, as with certain designer clothing.

NILS HOLGER MOORMANN

Hat man den Raum durch einen der schmalen Eingänge betreten, setzt sich der Zeltcharakter fort: vier große, helle, aufgespannte Schirme begrenzen den Raum nach oben und dienen zugleich als Befestigungsmöglichkeit für die sparsame, punktuelle Beleuchtung.

The area is accessible through one of the narrow entrances and maintains its tent-like character within: four large light-coloured opened-up umbrellas demarcate the top of the stand and simultaneously provide a support for the sparse, selective lighting.

Year	**2002**
Location	**Cologne**
Trade Fair	**International Furniture Fair**
Exhibitor	**Moormann Möbel Produktions- und Handels GmbH, Aschau i. Chiemgau**
Architect	**Moormann Möbel Produktions- und Handels GmbH, Aschau i. Chiemgau**
Size	**72 m²**
Realisation	**Moormann Möbel Produktions- und Handels GmbH, Aschau i. Chiemgau**

Ballspiel

Ball Game

Arno Design GmbH
für ellesse

Arno Design GmbH
for ellesse

Anlässlich der ispo 2002 gab es einen kompletten Relaunch der Marke ellesse. In diesem Zusammenhang wurde auch das Logo, das in den 70er-Jahren mit dem Einstieg in die Produktion von Tenniskleidung entstand, wieder mit neuem Wert bedacht. Dieses Logo in der Form eines Tennisballs führte zum dreidimensionalen Konzept der Standarchitektur, die an den Farben und Konturen des traditionellen „half-ball"-Logos ausgerichtet ist: vier übergroße, aufgeschnittene, weiße Tennisbälle stehen für die Sortimente Tennis, Ski, Sportschuhe und Freizeitkleidung, die auf arrangierten Büsten und Tableaus gezeigt werden.

On the occasion of ispo 2002 the ellesse brand was completely relaunched. In this context, the logo, which was created in the seventies when the company began producing tennis clothing, was also given new value. This logo in the form of a tennis ball led to the three-dimensional concept of the stand architecture that takes up the colours and contours of the traditional "half ball" logo: four oversized, cut-open, white tennis balls represent the tennis, ski, sports-shoe and leisure-wear collections that are displayed on arranged tailor's dummies and tableaux.

Sowohl die innere als auch die äußere Schalenoberfläche werden als Projektionsflächen genutzt: auf die äußere Schalenoberfläche werden Wasser- und Schneemotive projiziert, die inneren Oberflächen dienen der Produktvorstellung. Das Rückgrat des strahlend weißen Standes bildet eine geschwungene Wand, hinter der sich Räume für Lager, Logistik, Bewirtung und Besprechungen verbergen.

Both the inner and outer shells of the balls are used as projection surfaces: water and snow motives are projected onto the outer surfaces, whereas the inner surfaces are used for the product presentation. The backbone of the gleaming white stand forms a curved wall, behind which the rooms for storage, logistics, catering and meetings are concealed.

Vor der blauen Rück-
wand leuchtet die rot-
orange Wand, die
Besprechung, Lager,
Logistik und Bewirtung
abschirmt.

The radiant orange-
red wall in front of the
blue rear wall shields
the meeting, storage,
logistics and catering
areas.

Year	**2002**
Location	**Munich**
Trade Fair	**ispo**
Exhibitor	**ellesse International Ltd., London**
Architect	**Arno Design GmbH, Munich:** **Project Management: Detlef Biermann** **Architecture / Design: Mirka Nassiri,** **Peter Haberlander, Claus Neuleib**
Lighting	**Müllermusic, Cologne**
Size	**324 m²**
Realisation	**Arno Design GmbH, Munich**
Photos	**Frank Kotzerke, Munich**

Satelliten-Klassenzimmer
Satellite Classroom

designatics®
für „Schulen ans Netz"

designatics®
for "Schulen ans Netz"
(Internet for Schools)

„Schulen ans Netz" ist eine Initiative des Bundesministeriums
für Bildung und Forschung und der Deutschen Telekom AG.
Für eine Sonderschau auf der Bildungsmesse mussten mehr als
40 Einzelprojekte teilnehmender Schulen adäquat präsentiert
werden. Diese Projekte werden auf so genannten „Tafel-
satelliten" präsentiert, die modernste Computertechnik mit
einer klassischen Tafeloberfläche kombinieren, die von jeder
Schule frei gestaltbar ist. Sie sind um das Standinnere mit dem
Internet-Klassenzimmer, der Infotheke, der Lounge und der
Präsentationsbühne mit Zuschauerraum angeordnet. Diese
futuristischen, transluzenten Räume sind in Segmentbauweise
aus Acrylglas und pulverbeschichtetem Stahl gebaut.

Internet for Schools is an initiative of the Federal Ministry for
Education and Research and Deutsche Telekom AG. More than
40 individual projects by participating schools had to be suitably
presented for a special exhibition at the Education Trade Fair.
These projects are presented on so-called "blackboard satellites",
the lastest computer technology combined with a classic
blackboard surface that can be freely designed by each school.
They are arranged around the stand's interior with the internet
classroom, info stand, lounge and the presentation stage and
spectator area. These futuristic, translucent areas are constructed
of segments using acrylic glass and powder-coated steel.

Year	**2002**
Location	**Cologne**
Trade Fair	**Education Trade Fair**
Exhibitor	**Schulen ans Netz e.V., Bonn**
Architect	**designatics®, Cologne: Frank Hussong, Michael Kientzler, Daniela Reuter**
Lighting	**EMP EBI Media Productions GmbH**
Size	**620 m²**
Realisation	**designatics®**
Graphics / Communication	**CCM / designatics®**
Photos	**Martin Gaissert**

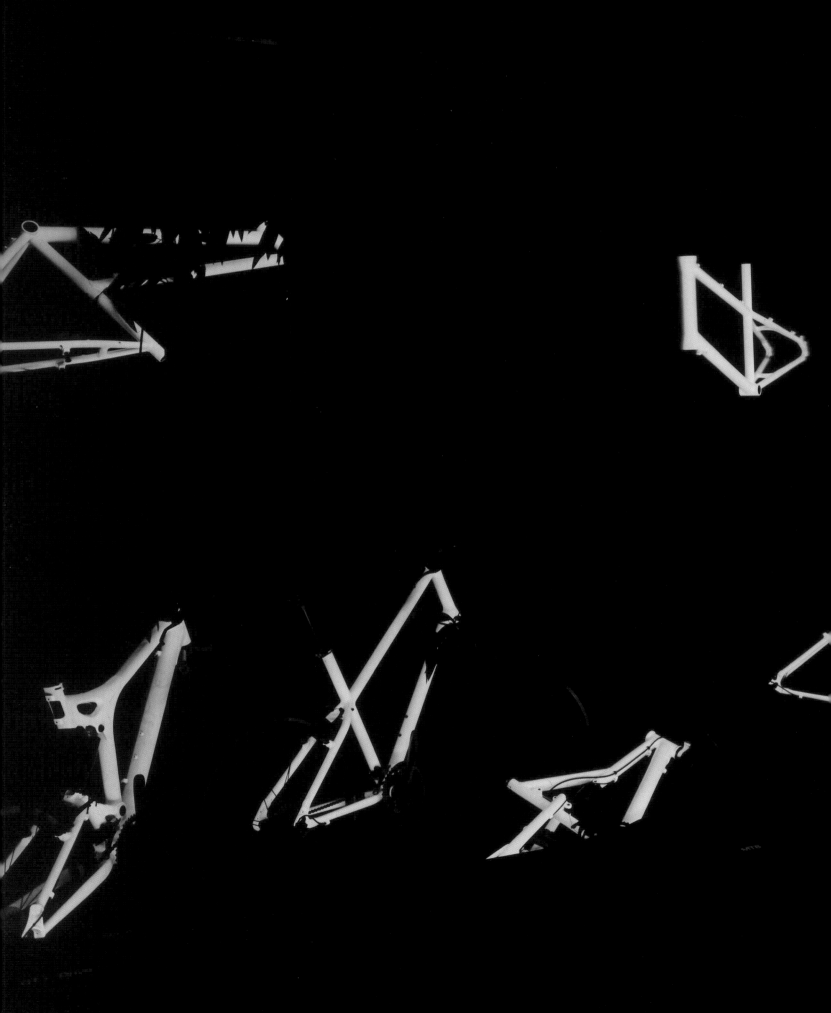

Röntgenbilder

X-Ray Images

Jörg Boner
für velo.com

Jörg Boner
for velo.com

Das Unternehmen velo.com ist ein Vertriebspool von drei innovativen Schweizer Fahrradmarken mit einer umfangreichen und vielfältigen Produktpalette. Für die Messe ist diese mit allen technischen Angaben im neu erstellten Katalog zu finden, dadurch mussten nicht alle angebotenen Modelle gezeigt werden.

Flankiert von drei Straßenlaternen (die für den letzten Messestand schon einmal eine wichtige Rolle spielten) steht ein kleiner Holzschuppen mit akzentuierter Front, dahinter ein weißer Kühlschrank und Bierzeltgarnituren für das Kundengespräch. Betritt der Besucher durch eine Schleuse das Innere, befindet er sich in einem komplett schwarzen Raum, an dessen Ende hinter einer 6 m langen, raumhohen Glasfront zehn mit selbstleuchtender Farbe lackierte Fahrradrahmen liegen und hängen. So wird das Produkt Fahrradrahmen zu einem geheimnisvollen, absurden, skelettartigen Reptil, das wie im Terrarium des Zoos hinter Glas die Besucher betrachtet und von ihnen als etwas völlig anderes wahrgenommen wird.

The company velo.com is a sales pool of three innovative Swiss bicycle brands with a wide, diverse product range. For the trade fair this range can be found in the newly created catalogue together with all the technical details, meaning that not all the models on offer have to be displayed.

Flanked by three street lanterns (which already played an important role for the last trade fair stand) is a small wooden shed with an accentuated front; behind this are a white fridge and biergarten trimmings for customer talks. Once the visitor has entered the interior through a double-door system, he finds himself in a pitch black room at the end of which 10 bicycle frames in fluorescent colours are lying or hanging behind a 6-metre-long, ceiling-high glass front. The bicycle frame as a product is thereby turned into a mysterious, absurd, skeletal reptile that is viewed by the visitor behind glass, like in a terrarium at the zoo, and seen in a completely different light.

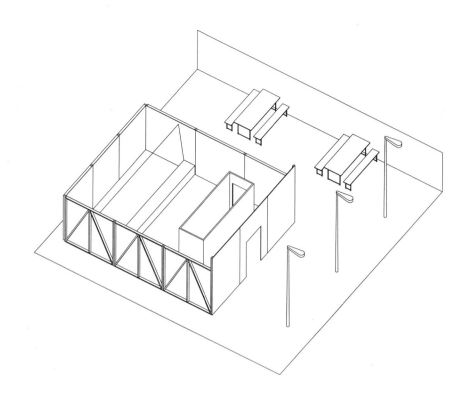

Year	**2002**
Location	**Zurich (CH)**
Trade Fair	**Bicycle Trade Fair**
Exhibitor	**velo.com, Schlieren (CH)**
Architect	**Jörg Boner, Zurich (CH)**
Lighting	**Deuber Lichttechnik, Lucern (CH)**
Size	**100 m²**
Realisation	**Troxler Innenausbau, Auw (CH)**
Graphics / Communication	**Jörg Boner, Zurich (CH)**
Photos	**Heinz Unger, Zurich (CH)**

Lichtskulptur
Light Sculpture

A.J. Kunzweiler GmbH
Eigenstand

A.J. Kunzweiler GmbH
Own Stand

Die milchigweiße Lichtskulptur des Messebauers Kunzweiler, die an einen überdimensionalen Buchstaben erinnert, zeigt, dass auch auf kleinstem Raum (32 m²) durchaus alle Funktionen eines großen Messestandes abgedeckt sein und dabei auch noch abwechslungsreiche Räume gebildet werden können. Mit dem Slogan „Freiräume für Phantasien schaffen – Ideen verwirklichen" sollten Unternehmen angesprochen werden, die kundenspezifische Lösungen für ihre Messeauftritte fordern und durch ihren Messeauftritt ihre Corporate Identity visualisieren und kommunizieren wollen.

Der teils offene, teils geschlossene Stand besteht aus einheitlich weißem, teils opakem, teils transparentem Material mit vielen hinterleuchteten Bauteilen (Lichtboden, Lichttreppe, Lichthandlauf, etc.). Ein kleiner Besprechungsraum mit Videowand im Obergeschoss bildet einen – ebenfalls leuchtenden – Ausguck.

The milky-white light sculpture by the trade fair constructor Kunzweiler, which calls to mind an oversized letter, demonstrates that all the functions of a large trade fair stand can be perfectly covered and at the same time diverse areas created in the smallest of spaces (32m²). The slogan "Creating room for fantasy, realising ideas" is aimed at companies that call for client-specific solutions for their trade fair appearances and also want to use their trade fair appearance to visualise and convey their corporate identity.

The partly open, partly closed stand consists of a uniformly white, partly opaque, partly transparent material with numerous backlit components (floor, stairs, handrail, etc.). A small meeting area with a video wall on the upper level forms a lookout, likewise illuminated.

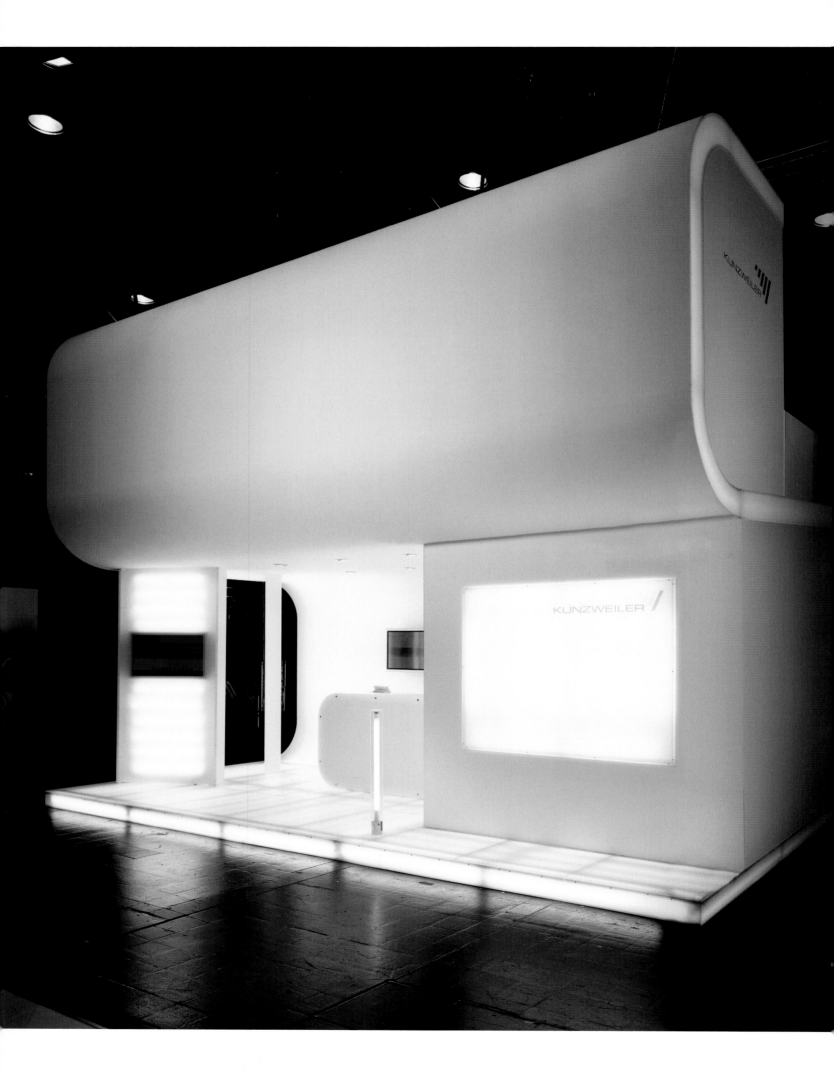

Wie in der Filmarchitektur eines Science-Fiction strahlen die hinterleuchteten Bauteile dem Besucher entgegen.

The backlit components shine out at the visitor, like in the architecture of a science-fiction film.

Year	**2002**
Location	**Duesseldorf**
Trade Fair	**Euroshop**
Exhibitor	**A.J. Kunzweiler GmbH, Weil am Rhein**
Architect	**Wolfgang Kunzweiler, Weil am Rhein**
Lighting	**A.J. Kunzweiler GmbH, Weil am Rhein**
Size	**32 m²**
Realisation	**A.J. Kunzweiler GmbH, Weil am Rhein**
Graphics / Communication	**Wolfgang Kunzweiler / ProConception Image Productions L.A.**
Photos	**MP Photography**

Ballonskulptur
Balloon Sculpture

D'Art Design Gruppe
Eigenstand

D'Art Design Group
Own Stand

Ohne ein eigentliches Produkt stellt die D'Art Design Gruppe in einer temporären Architektur Dienstleistung vor / aus: Entwicklung und Realisierung von Lösungen für die gesamte Bandbreite von Kommunikation mit dem Schwerpunkt Shop- und Messedesign. Es entstand ein an eine Installation von Flatz auf der Documenta IX erinnernder Punchingball-Wald, der aber hier aus 154 leichten, luftgefüllten weißen Ballons besteht. Die 154 verschiedenen aufgedruckten Wörter bilden Assoziationsketten zum Spannungsfeld „Inhalt versus Oberfläche".

Nach außen sieht man ein halbtransparentes Volumen aus Hüllen, dessen Inhalt man erst auf die Spur kommt, wenn man sich spielerisch seinen Weg durch die Ballons bahnt. Man findet im Zentrum einen Tisch als Projektionsfläche für atmosphärische Filme, eine Theke mit Laptop und essbaren, weißen kleinen Giveaways mit Aufschriften in Form von Beipackzetteln.

With no actual product, the D'Art Design Group presents and exhibits a service in a temporary architecture: the development and realisation of solutions for the complete spectrum of communication with particular emphasis on shop and trade fair design. A punching-ball forest was created – reminiscent of an installation by Flatz at the Documenta IX – here, however, comprising 154 light, inflated white balloons each printed with a different word, together forming chains of association with the point at issue "content versus surface".

From the outside a semitransparent volume of skins is visible, the content of which only becomes apparent when the visitors playfully fight their way through the balloons. In the centre is a table, onto whose surface atmospheric films are projected, and a bar with a laptop and small edible white give-aways carrying labels in the form of dosage instructions.

An Terminals (Spielstationen) im Ballonwald kann der Besucher mittels Joystick ein virtuelles Modell des realen Messestandes erkunden und Bilder, Texte und Filme zu Projekten abrufen. Die Assoziation „Wald" wurde unter anderem durch die subtile Beschallung des Standes hervorgerufen (Grillenzirpen, Möwengeschrei, Fluggeräusche von Insekten etc.).

At the terminals (play stations) in the forest of balloons the visitor can explore a virtual model of the real trade fair stand using a joystick and call up images, texts and films relating to company projects. Among other things, the subtle use of background noises (the chirping of crickets, screeching of gulls, sounds of insects in flight, etc.) help to conjure up "forest" associations.

Ähneln die frei beweglichen Ballons von weitem noch einer großen Wolke, können aus der Nähe dann auch die aufgedruckten Worte gelesen werden.

From a distance the freely moving balloons resemble a large cloud, whereas close up the words printed on them become legible.

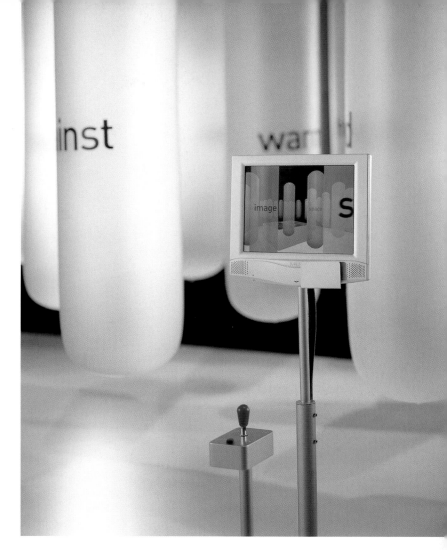

Year	**2002**
Location	**Duesseldorf**
Trade Fair	**Euroshop**
Exhibitor	**D'Art Design Gruppe, Neuss**
Architect	**D'Art Design Gruppe, Neuss:** **Karin Blanke, Conny Cavlek, Silke Eimanns, Jochen Höffler, Dominik Hof, Guido Mamczur, Jonas Reinsch**
Lighting	**D'Art Design Gruppe, Neuss**
Size	**204 m²**
Realisation	**ACES GmbH, Neuss**
Photos	**H. G. Esch, Cologne**

Fliesenwände

Tiled Walls

Design Company / Sony Deutschland
Eigenstand

Design Company / Sony Germany
Own Stand

Auf Waschbetonplatten stehen fünf große parallele Wandscheiben mit Maßen von 5 x 6 m, die mit schwarzen Fliesen beklebt sind und mit dieser außergewöhnlichen Materialsprache für das unverwechselbare Erscheinungsbild des Messestandes sorgen, auf dem sich die Design Company mit einem ihrer Kunden, Sony Deutschland, präsentiert.

In die Außenseite der schwarzen Wände sind Schaufenster integriert, in denen die Branchen- und Dekothemen der Design Company kommuniziert werden. Im Mittelpunkt der Präsentation steht eine Ausstellung über Projekte, die auf Sony-Plasmascreens gezeigt wird.

Five large parallel wall panels measuring 5 x 6 metres are positioned on exposed aggregate concrete slabs. The panels are covered in black tiles and with this unusual material are responsible for the unmistakable appearance of the trade fair stand on which the Design Company is presented together with one of its clients, Sony Germany.

Display windows are integrated into the outside of the black walls in which the business and décor themes of the Design Company are communicated. Central to the presentation is an exhibition on projects that are shown on Sony plasma screens.

DESIGN COMPANY
MESSE- U. SHOPDESIGN

Die obere Ebene des zweigeschossigen Standes dient als Kommunikationsbereich, der sich durch zusätzliche Materialien von der kühlen Erscheinung der äußeren Hülle absetzt.

The carpeted lounge in the upper storey with its leather armchairs and wooden furniture contrasts with the cold, black, smooth walls.

Year	**2002**
Location	**Duesseldorf**
Trade Fair	**Euroshop**
Exhibitor	**Design Company GmbH, Munich** **Cooperation: Sony Deutschland, Cologne**
Architect	**Design Company GmbH, Munich:** **Concept: Uwe Ansorge** **Design: Hubert Grothaus**
Size	**120 m², 70 m² Topdeck**
Realisation	**Tom Pschorr GmbH, Hofheim**
Graphics / Communication	**Design Company GmbH, Munich**
Photos	**Michael Ingenweyen, Munich**

Geschenkverpackt
Gift Wrapped

Leitner GmbH
Eigenstand

Leitner GmbH
Own Stand

Wie eine saubere Baustelle, deren Fassade gerade hergerichtet wird, steht der mit Folie wie ein Geschenk verpackte, zweigeschossige Stand weithin sichtbar in der Messehalle. Er bildet einen spannenden, unprätentiösen Kontrast zu den formalen und funktionalen Neuentwicklungen zweier Leitner Raumsysteme: des Doppelstocks L10 und des Systems L26 „Der kleine Leitner".

Als Rückzugsbereich und gleichzeitig Ausguck dient in einem der Stand-„Viertel" der L10 Doppelstock. Auf der gegenüberliegenden Standseite wird L26, das als Messesystem für kleine Stände konzipiert ist, ausführlich präsentiert. Es basiert auf dem 30-mm-Würfel, der seit 40 Jahren als das Verbindungselement der Leitner GmbH bekannt ist. Horizontale und vertikale Profilrahmen für das Standskelett werden mit Spinnacker- oder Spanplattenpaneelen gefüllt.

Wrapped like a gift in plastic foil, this two-storey stand has a far-reaching impact in the trade fair hall and resembles a clean building site, whose facade has just been done up. It forms a dramatic, unpretentious contrast to the formal, functional new developments of two Leitner spatial systems: the double-storey L10 and the "Mini Leitner" L26 system.

In one "quarter" of the stand the double-storey L10 functions as a private area of retreat, doubling up as a lookout. On the opposite side of the stand the L26, which was conceived as a trade fair system for small stands, is presented in detail. It is based on the 30-mm cube, which is well known as the connecting element used by Leitner GmbH for the past 40 years. Horizontal and vertical sectional frames for the stand's skeletal structure are filled in with spinnaker or chipboard panels.

Das dezente Leitner-Logo und der entsprechende Barcode auf der Folienhaut sind die einzigen Hinweise auf den Aussteller.

The discreet Leitner logo and the corresponding barcode on the outer transparent skin are the only references to the exhibitor.

In jedem der hier aufgebauten Raumabteile finden sich andere Zusatzelemente: Regale, Container, Spinde, Messeküche usw. Eine neue Tischgeneration und Messestand-Container für L+ ergänzen die ausgestellten Produkte und finden ebenfalls ihren Raum in der strengen Geometrie des Standes.

Each of the assembled spatial compartments houses additional elements: shelves, containers, lockers, exhibition kitchen, etc. A new table generation and trade fair stand container for L+ complement the exhibited products and also find their place in the strict geometry of the stand.

Innen umlaufendes,
fast endloses Fotoband
mit Darstellung der
Systeme und des kul-
turellen Engagements
der Leitner GmbH.

The almost endless
band of photos
circling the interior,
which portray Leitner
GmbH's systems and,
above all, cultural
commitments.

Year	**2002**
Location	**Duesseldorf**
Trade Fair	**Euroshop**
Exhibitor	**Leitner GmbH, Waiblingen**
Architect	**Leitner GmbH, Waiblingen:** **Leitner Planungsabteilung**
Lighting	**Zumtobel Staff** **Leitner GmbH**
Size	**300 m²**
Realisation	**Leitner GmbH, Waiblingen:** **Leitner Services GmbH**
Graphics / Communication	**Brasilhaus, Bremen**
Photos	**Frank Erber, Ostfildern**

Vornehme Zurückhaltung
Elegant Understatement

Gaggenau Design
für Gaggenau Hausgeräte

Gaggenau Design
for Gaggenau Hausgeräte

In diesem nach außen sehr geschlossenen Messestand sieht man zuerst nur die Flächen der Präsentationskörper und kein Produkt. Erst wenn man die Freifläche mit der Infotheke durchschritten hat, gelangt man durch einen überdachten Gang mit hohen Wandscheiben in den Ausstellungs- oder aber Besprechungs-/Bewirtungsbereich. Im Ausstellungsbereich stehen die Produkte im Mittelpunkt. Deshalb werden die hochwertigen Küchen-einbaugeräte auch nicht in realen Küchensituationen, sondern in skulpturalen weißen Körpern präsentiert.

At first only the surfaces of the presentation bodies, rather than any actual products, are visible in this trade fair stand due to its closed appearance on the outside. To reach the covered-over passageway with high wall panels in the exhibition or meeting/catering area, the visitor first has to walk through the open space accommodating the info stand. The focal point in the exhibition area is the products. For this reason the high-quality fitted-kitchen appliances are not presented in real kitchen situations, but rather in sculptural white bodies.

Der Zugang zu dem geschlossen wirkenden Besprechungs- /
Bewirtungsbereich wird durch metallbeschichtete Wände, die
leicht versetzt angeordnet sind, ermöglicht. Grafik wird auf die-
sem Stand nur sehr sparsam eingesetzt. Die im Gang auf den
Wandscheiben projizierten Filme zeigen Menschen beim
Kochen.

The apparently closed meeting/catering area can be accessed
through metal-coated walls arranged slightly obliquely. There
is minimal use of graphics on this stand. The films projected
onto the wall panels in the passageway show people cooking.

Ein 3-Sterne-Koch
zeigt die Geräte in
Benutzung.

A 3-star chef demon-
strates the appliances.

Year	**2002**
Location	**Berlin**
Trade Fair	**Hometech**
Exhibitor	**Gaggenau Hausgeräte GmbH, Munich**
Architect	**Gaggenau Design, Munich** **Project Management:** **Anne Bergner, Munich** **Team: Sven Baacke, Reinhard Segers**
Lighting	**Imagic Production GmbH,** **Taufkirchen / Vils**
Size	**600 m²**
Realisation	**Altmann Messe- und Ladenbau GmbH,** **Bönnigheim**
Graphics / Communication	**Gaggenau Design, Munich:** **Anne Bergner, Reinhard Segers**
Photos	**Monika Höfler, Munich**

security at work.

Mehr Sicherheit in der Banknotenbearbeitung
Enhanced security for banknote processing

Sicherheitsstreifen
Security Bands

designafairs exhibition services GmbH
für Giesecke & Devrient

designafairs exhibition services GmbH
for Giesecke & Devrient

Giesecke & Devrient gilt als innovativer Technologieführer im Bereich der Sicherheitstechnologie. Unter Beachtung visueller Verbindungen zu den vorherigen Messeauftritten wurden für das Standmotto „security at work" Assoziationen zum Thema Sicherheit augenzwinkernd umgesetzt. So weisen „Wasserwände" als Abschluss an den beiden Querseiten auf Wasserzeichen hin. Als Wasserkreislauf in einem Baukörper im Innern des Standes wird die Kontinuität der Sicherheitslösungen dargestellt, und das durch Bänder aufgelöste Volumen des Standes symbolisiert Barcodes. Auf diese Bänder projizierte, bewegte Slogans stellen Fragen an die Sicherheit.

Zwischen eingeschobenen Scheiben findet die eigentliche Produktpräsentation auf mobilen Präsentationsplätzen mit Flachbildschirmen statt.

Giesecke & Devrient are well known as innovative leaders in the field of security technology. Picking up on visual associations with their previous trade fair appearances, associations with the security theme are brought light-heartedly into play for the stand's motto "security at work". "Water walls", for example, closing in the two short sides, are a reference to watermarks; the continuity of the security solutions is represented as a water cycle in a structure in the stand's interior, and the volume of the stand is broken up by bands to symbolise barcodes.

Moving slogans posing security-related questions are projected onto these bands. The actual product presentation takes place at mobile product presentation stations with flat-screens, positioned between panels.

Eine Produktneuheit, Numeron, wird auf einer Drehscheibe im Cash-Center in Szene gesetzt.

A new product, Numeron, is staged on a turntable in the cash centre.

Year	**2002**
Location	**Hanover**
Trade Fair	**CeBIT**
Exhibitor	**Giesecke & Devrient GmbH, Munich**
Architect	**designafairs exhibition services GmbH, Erlangen** **Concept, Design & Architecture:** **Ulrich Kostka** **Project Management: Stefan Dischl** **Graphics: Ralf Weidemeier**
Lighting	**Pre-View Andreas Schlonsok, Hanover**
Size	**595 m²**
Realisation	**Trade fair construction and completion of interiors: Fink Holz-Metall, Erlangen** **Structural steel engineering:** **Ernst Hugo Stahlbau, Hanover**
Graphics / Communication	**AV: BTS, Munich** **Graphics: PWR Communication, Fürth** **Communication: Rempen & Partner, Munich**
Photos	**Rottmann Werbefotografie, Nuremberg:** **Maren Rottmann & Astrid Paatsch**

Farbenstadt
Colour City

Arno Design GmbH
für Sto

Arno Design GmbH
for Sto

Nur im Innern entfaltet der dreiteilige Messestand der Sto AG seine Farbigkeit; von außen ist er grau und mit Ausnahme der Hausfarbe Gelb weist auch nichts auf die Farben innen hin. Dort betritt der Besucher eine Stadt – sehr offen und gleichzeitig intim – mit Räumen zur Produktinformation und zum Verweilen, einem bestuhlten Platz, der Treff- und Informationspunkt ist und Werbeflächen mit Projektionen auf transparenten Wänden zum Thema Farbe.

Themenkuben in Alurahmenbauweise mit beidseitiger Beplankung zeigen verschiedene Produktschwerpunkte (so z. B. die Themen „Fassade" oder „Innenraum"), in einem eigenen Kubus wird der neue Farbfächer vorgestellt, zwei weitere Kuben dienen der Präsentation der Produktpalette. Mit nur vier Farben (Orange, Weinrot, Pink, Senfgelb) aus dem neuen Sto-Farbfächer, der erlebbar gemacht werden sollte, entstehen an jeder Stelle des Messestandes neue Stimmungen.

The colourfulness of Sto AG's three-part trade fair stand only emerges in the interior; on the outside the stand is grey and, with the exception of the house colour yellow, shows no signs of the colours within. Inside, the visitor enters a city – very open yet intimate at the same time – with areas for product information or for relaxation, a seated area serving as a meeting and information point, and advertising space with colour-related images projected onto transparent walls.

Theme cubes with an aluminium frame construction and planking on either side show various product highlights (e.g. the "facade" or "interiors" themes). The new colour range is introduced in a separate cube; two further cubes serve as presentation areas for the product range. A new mood is created at every point of the trade fair stand by using only four colours (orange, bordeaux, pink and mustard) from the new Sto colour range for the visitor to experience.

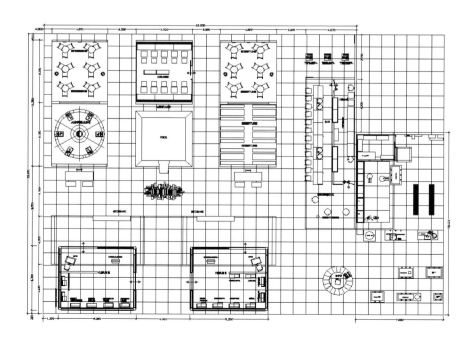

Grundriss

Plan

Die hinterleuchteten
Kuben, die Produkt-
informationen be-
inhalten, durchdringen
die großen Tore im
Gelb der Hausfarbe.

The backlit cubes,
containing product
information penetrate
the large entrance-
ways in the yellow
house colour.

Year	**2002**
Location	**Munich**
Trade Fair	**Farbe**
Exhibitor	**Sto AG, Stühlingen**
Architect	**Arno Design GmbH, Munich:** **Project Management: Karsten Reinhold,** **Architecture / Design: Claus Neuleib**
Lighting	**Arno Design GmbH, Munich**
Size	**704 m²**
Realisation	**Arno Design GmbH, Munich**
Photos	**Frank Kotzerke, Munich**

Licht-Trichter
Light Funnels

Kurz und Partner Architekten
für Mercedes-Benz

Kurz und Partner Architekten
for Mercedes-Benz

Hauptelement der Gestaltung dieses Messestandes ist das wolkenförmige Deckensegel, das über einem amöbenförmigen Präsentationspodest schwebt. Beleuchtete Stofftrichter durchdringen dieses Deckensegel, zonieren und begrenzen den Stand und setzen Akzente auf die Fahrzeug-Highlights. Zusätzlich bieten die Trichter Projektionsfläche für die bewegte Grafik.

Dieser skulpturale Stand mit seiner eigenwilligen Formgebung – unterstützt durch eine Geräusch- und Klangkulisse – ist die Bühne, auf der dem Besucher die Markenwerte sinnlich vermittelt werden sollen. Die ausgestellten Autos werden zu den Akteuren in der Gesamtinszenierung.

The main design element of this trade fair stand is the wavelike sail suspended from the ceiling above an amoeba-shaped presentation platform. Illuminated fabric funnels penetrate this sail, zoning and marking the boundaries of the stand and accentuating the vehicle highlights. In addition, the moving graphics are projected onto the surface of these funnels.

This sculptural stand with its unconventional design – reinforced by a backdrop of sounds and tones – is the stage on which the brand values are meant to be sensorially conveyed to the visitor. The exhibited vehicles become actors in the overall staging.

Das Kommunikations-
konzept bezieht auch
Bewegung und Klang
mit ein: die Lichtsäulen
werden mittels be-
wegter Projektionen
mit Typografie bespielt
und von abstrakten
Klangcollagen unter-
malt.

The communication
concept also includes
movement and sound:
Moving graphics are
projected onto the light
columns and abstract
sound collages provide
background noise.

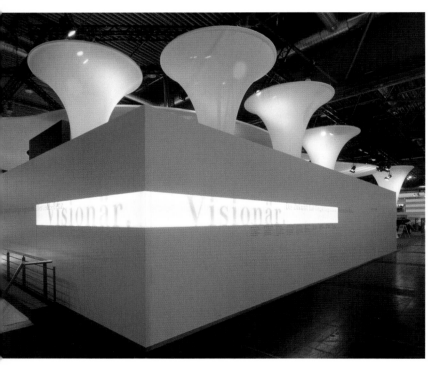

Year	**2002**
Location	**Leipzig**
Trade Fair	**Automobil International – AMI**
Exhibitor	**DaimlerChrysler AG, Berlin / Mercedes-Benz**
Complete Organisation	**Vertikal Marketing Events, Urbach**
Architect	**Kurz und Partner Architekten, Urbach**
Lighting	**TLD-Lichttechnik GmbH, Riemerling**
Graphics / Communication	**Büro für Gestaltung, Kommunikation und Kultur Ine Ilg, Aalen**
Size	**990 m²**
Realisation	**Raumtechnik Messebau & Event Marketing GmbH, Ostfildern-Ruit**
Photos	**Andreas Keller, Altdorf**

Smarte Welle
Smart Waves

Kurz und Partner Architekten
für smart

Kurz und Partner Architekten
for smart

Im Gegensatz zu den Messeauftritten der anderen Daimler-Chrysler Marken ähneln sich die Designkonzepte der Messeauftritte der Marke smart noch sehr, da die Marke noch nicht so verankert ist. Da extrem trendorientierte Markenwerte betont werden sollen, wurde die Welle als Ausdruck für Dynamik und Mobilität gewählt.

Ein wellenförmiges Band in hochglanzlackiertem Weiß mit hinterleuchteten Vorderkanten strafft sich zwischen den Standkanten. Im eingeschossigen Bereich bildet es die Abdeckung der Nebenräume, im ebenerdigen Bereich ist es Präsentationsfläche für das Highlight. Ein zusätzliches Podest in der gleichen Farbe dient als Fläche für Fahrzeugpräsentationen und zusätzliche Aktionen.

In contrast to the trade fair appearances of the other Daimler-Chrysler brands, the design concepts of the trade fair appearances of the smart brand are still very similar since the brand is not yet as established. Since extremely trend-orientated brand values are to be emphasised, the wave was selected to express dynamism and mobility.

A wavelike band with a glossy white finish and back-lit edges spans the length of the stand. It covers the side rooms in the single-storey area, whereas at ground level it serves as a presentation area for the highlight. A second platform in the same colour serves as an area for vehicle presentation and for additional promotions.

Auch die Möblierung
mit den abgerundeten
Ecken passt in das
Retro-Erscheinungsbild
des Standes.

The furnishings with
their rounded edges
are also suited to the
stand's retro-look.

Year	**2002**
Location	**Leipzig**
Trade Fair	**Automobil International – AMI**
Exhibitor	**DaimlerChrysler AG, Berlin / smart**
Complete Organisation	**Vertikal Marketing Events, Urbach**
Architect	**Kurz und Partner Architekten, Urbach**
Lighting	**TLD-Lichttechnik GmbH, Riemerling**
Graphics / Communication	**Scharein & Partner, Frankfurt a. M.**
Size	**240 m²**
Realisation	**Messeprojekt GmbH, Leipzig**
Photos	**Andreas Keller, Altdorf**

Heiter bewölkt
Bright and Cloudy

Atelier Markgraph
für Messe Frankfurt am Main

Atelier Markgraph
for Messe Frankfurt am Main

Die Sonderschau „Constructing Atmospheres" entstand anlässlich der neu integrierten Klimamesse „Aircontec" zur light + building. Die Sonderschau, deren Highlight die Konstruktion einer meteorologisch echten Wolke ist, widmet sich der menschlichen Wahrnehmung von Raum und Klima.

Der gesamte Kuppelbau der Galleria zwischen Halle 8 und 9 ist mit einer 400 m³ großen, künstlichen Wolke gefüllt, die mehrmals täglich aus Luftschichten unterschiedlicher Feuchtigkeit und Temperatur generiert wird. Abends wird aus der „Experimental Cloud" mit einer Licht- und Klanginstallation über einem Club ein Beitrag der Messe zum Licht-Kultur-Festival „Luminale".

The special exhibition "Constructing Atmospheres" originated on the occasion of the newly integrated trade fair for air conditioning, "Aircontec" at light + building. The special exhibition, the highlight of which is the construction of a meteorologically authentic cloud, is devoted to the human perception of space and climate.

The entire domed construction of the galleria between halls 8 and 9 is filled with a 400-m³ artificial cloud, which is generated several times a day from air strata of varying humidity and temperature. In the evenings the experimental cloud with a light and sound installation above a club is a contribution by the trade fair to the "Luminale" Festival of Light and Culture.

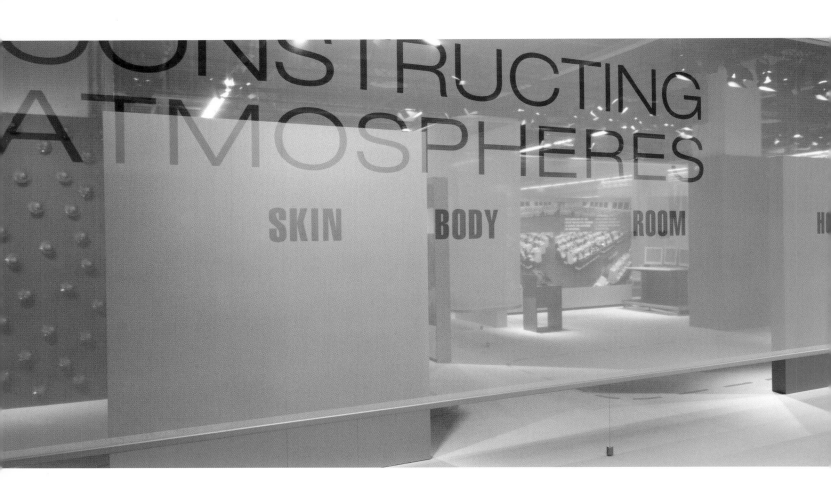

CONSTRUCTING
ATMOSPHERES

SKIN   BODY   ROOM   H

Die eigentliche Ausstellung mit ihren acht thematischen Bereichen ist umhüllt von transparenten, schwebenden Gazen. Auf einem Parcours erkundet der Besucher anhand von spektakulären Exponaten, interaktiven Experimenten und detaillierter Information interessante Fakten und Themenstellungen von der Hautzelle bis zum Universum. Dabei dienen stark farbige, monochrome Körper als Wegeführung, Grafik- und Exponatträger.

The actual exhibition with its eight thematic areas is shrouded in pieces of transparent suspended gauze. Along a pathway, the visitors investigate interesting facts and problematic subjects, ranging from skin cells to the universe, with the aid of spectacular exhibits, interactive experiments and detailed information. Intense-coloured monochrome bodies act as guides for the visitor and are also vehicles for conveying graphics and displaying exhibits.

Am Abend wird der Cloud Club unter der Wolke mit seinem ausgesuchten Musikprogramm und den speziellen Cocktails zu einer temporären Institution des Frankfurter Nachtlebens.

In the evenings the Cloud Club beneath the cloud, with its selected music programme and special cocktails, is transformed into a temporary institution of Frankfurt's night life.

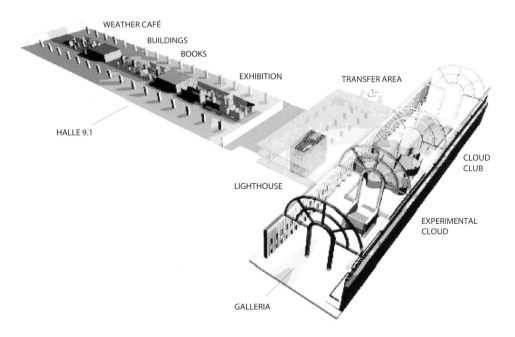

WEATHER CAFÉ

BUILDINGS

BOOKS

EXHIBITION

TRANSFER AREA

HALLE 9.1

LIGHTHOUSE

CLOUD CLUB

EXPERIMENTAL CLOUD

GALLERIA

Year	**2002**
Location	**Frankfurt a. M.**
Trade Fair	**light + building**
Exhibitor	**Messe Frankfurt GmbH, Frankfurt a. M.**
Architect	**Architecture, Design, Communication and Complete Management: Atelier Markgraph GmbH, Frankfurt a. M. Art Direction / Graphic Design: Janós Déri, Frankfurt a. M. Illustration: Damir Tomas, Frankfurt a. M.**
Lighting	**Design "Experimental Cloud": Atelier Markgraph GmbH, Frankfurt a. M. with: Study Programme "Lighting Design", FH Hildesheim Procon Multimedia AG, Hamburg**
Realisation	**CL Veranstaltungsservice, Flörsheim / Freisteel, Reichelsheim Graphic Production: Messegrafik & Messebau Schreiber, Oberursel / Procédés Chénel Werbegesellschaft mbH, Lemwerder Technical Realisation "Experimental Cloud": Transsolar Energietechnik GmbH, Schwäbisch Gmünd Sound "Experimental Cloud", "Cloud Club": Schleuse 15, Frankfurt a. M. Sound Exhibition "Constructing Atmospheres": Georg Stummer, Frankfurt a. M. Sound Engineering: Neumann & Müller GmbH, Wendlingen Climate Equipment "Experimental Cloud": R+S Reparatur und Service Haustechnik GmbH, Mettmann Media: AV Technik Vertriebs GmbH & Co. KG, Hamburg**
Photos	**Andreas Keller, Altdorf Damir Tomas, Frankfurt a. M. Jürgen Zeller, Frankfurt a. M.**

Lunis_R

Lunis_E

Lunis

compact downlight

Reflektorleuchte

Lichtstadt
City of Lights

Atelier Brückner
für Siteco

Atelier Brückner
for Siteco

Die Leuchtkuben des letzten Standes wurden zu einer Stadt
mit Türmen aus Licht weiterentwickelt, die konsequent zum
Standinnern geöffnet sind, nach außen aber als geschlossene
Kuben erscheinen.

Die mit transluzenter Folie bespannten Konstruktionselemente
leuchten, von innen angestrahlt, in unterschiedlichen, ständig
wechselnden, zeitlich vorprogrammierten Farbwechseln.
Diese Lichtstimmungen zeigen den Raum einmal in strahlender,
weißer Klarheit, dann wieder in kristallin schimmerndem,
rätselhaftem Blau.

The light cubes of the last stand have been developed into a
city with towers of light; the sides of the cubes facing the
stand's interior are invariably open, whereas from the outside
the cubes have a closed appearance.

The construction elements, covered in translucent plastic film,
are lit from the inside with various alternating colours using
a pre-programmed timer. According to these alternating light
moods, the space may be shown in a clear bright white or a
crystalline shimmering indeterminate blue.

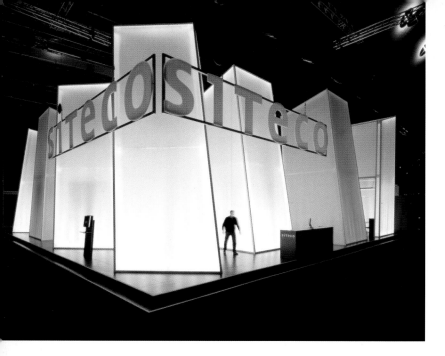

Durch die wechseln-
den Lichtstimmungen
bilden die verzerrten
textilen Türme ein sich
ständig veränderndes
Ensemble.

On account of the
changing light moods,
the distorted textile
towers form an ever-
changing ensemble.

Elf dieser acht Meter hohen begehbaren Türme bieten innen
Präsentationsräume für einzelne Produkte und Produktgruppen
von Innen- und Außenleuchten. Zwischen den Türmen bilden
sich Straßenschluchten und Plätze; Orte für Begegnungen,
Information und Gespräche.

In bewusstem Kontrast zu den leuchtenden Türmen steht der
sehr dunkle Boden und auch die übrige Standeinrichtung.

Eleven of these 8-metre-high accessible towers house internal
presentation areas for individual internal and external lighting
products and product groups. Narrow passageways and squares
are formed between the towers-places to meet, exchange
information and talk.

The very dark floor, together with the rest of the stand's
furnishings, presents a deliberate contrast to the illuminated
towers.

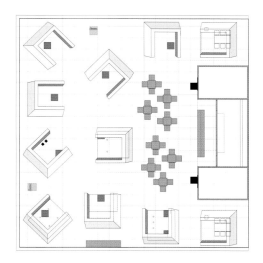

Grundriss

Plan

Year	**2002**
Location	**Frankfurt a. M.**
Trade Fair	**light + building**
Exhibitor	**Siteco Beleuchtungstechnik GmbH, Traunreut**
Architect	**Atelier Brückner, Stuttgart:** **Project Management: Dominik Hegemann** **Project Architect: Sayman Bostanci** **Team: Lars Jürgens, Dirk Schubert**
Lighting	**Concept: Atelier Brückner, Stuttgart** **Realisation: Siteco Beleuchtungstechnik GmbH, Traunreut**
Size	**420 m²**
Realisation	**Display International, Würselen**
Graphics / Communication	**Atelier Brückner, Stuttgart:** **Team: Sabine Binder, Birgit Kölz**
Photos	**Bernd Eidenmüller** **Victor S. Brigola, Stuttgart**

Kubenkomposition
Cube Composition

Zumtobel Staff
Eigenstand

Zumtobel Staff
Own Stand

Schon aus der Ferne werden die Besucher durch das Kernstück des Standes, die imposanten, 4 m hohen und 20 m langen Active Light Walls, angezogen. Durch gesteuerte Veränderungen der Intensität und Farbe ihres Lichts entsteht eine Atmosphäre, in der Verstand, Sinne und Gefühle des Besuchers angesprochen werden.

In schlichten und doch auffälligen Kuben wird gezeigt, wie sich in allen Anwendungsbereichen professioneller Gebäudebeleuchtung mit Active Light arbeiten lässt und wie sich mit den Produkten von Zumtobel Staff Erlebniswelten schaffen lassen. Das Licht selbst ist integrales Element der Raumgestaltung und Architektur. Es wird demonstriert, was damit bewirkt werden kann, vom Lichtrausch bis zur subtilen Beleuchtung, vom intensiven Farbspiel bis zu kaltem Schein. Der Stand ist Bühne, auf der Licht inszeniert und damit erlebbar wird und auf der die Besucher zu Akteuren werden.

Even from afar, the visitors are attracted by the stand's centrepiece, the imposing 4-metre high and 20-metre long Active Light walls. Through controlled changes in the intensity and colour of the light, an atmosphere is created that addresses the visitors' mind, senses and feelings.

In simple yet outstanding cubes it is demonstrated how Active Light can be worked with in all areas of application of professional building lighting and how theme worlds can be created using the Zumtobel Staff products. The light itself is an integral element of the spatial design and architecture. We are given a demonstration of what can be achieved with it: from dynamic to subtle lighting, from an intensive colour show to cold light. The stand is the stage on which the light setting is presented as an experience and on which the visitors form the cast.

In den einzelnen
Kuben aus Ahorn und
Aluminium und den
dazwischenliegenden
Korridoren werden die
verschiedenen Produk-
te und deren Wirkung
vorgeführt.

The various products
and their effects are
presented in the indi-
vidual cubes made of
maple and aluminium
and in the corridors in
between.

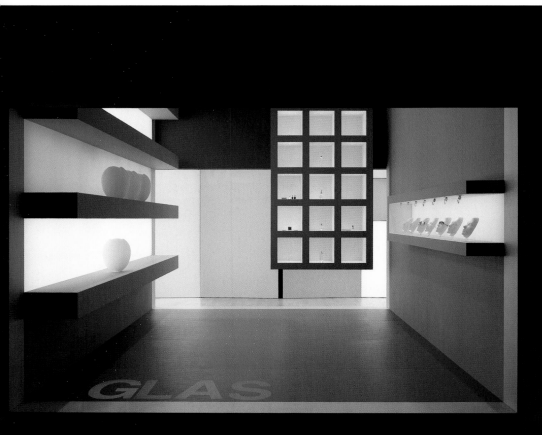

Year	2002
Location	Frankfurt a. M.
Trade Fair	light + building
Exhibitor	Zumtobel Staff GmbH, Dornbirn (A)
Architect	Messebau Zumtobel Staff GmbH, Dornbirn (A)
Lighting	Zumtobel Staff GmbH, Dornbirn (A)
Size	600 m²
Realisation	Messebau Zumtobel Staff GmbH, Dornbirn (A)
Photos	Zumtobel Staff GmbH, Dornbirn (A)

Wolkenspiel
Cloud Play

Zeeh, Bahls & Partner Design GmbH
für Siemens Automation & Drives

Zeeh, Bahls & Partner Design GmbH
for Siemens Automation & Drives

Schon von weitem sichtbar sind drei verschiedenfarbig, individuell beleuchtete Raumobjekte, die über dem Stand zu schweben scheinen. In der Ruhe dieser wolkenähnlichen, begehbaren Körper, die auf einer Höhe von 4,20 m mit einem 80 m langen, stählernen Steg verbunden sind, werden die Kernbotschaften der einzelnen Geschäftsfelder auf einem „Pfad der Sinne" vermittelt. Wandernde Videobilder und Botschaften werden mit beweglichen Laserbeamern, die sich um 320 Grad drehen können, direkt auf die gekrümmte Membranoberfläche projiziert. Als zusätzliche Bildträger sind HoloProscheiben in die Wolken eingehängt.

The three different-coloured individually illuminated structures that appear to be hovering above the stand are visible from afar. In the calm of these cloud-like accessible bodies, which are connected at a height of 4.2 metres by an 80-metre-long steel bridge, the key communications of the individual business areas are conveyed on a "pathway of the senses". Moving video images and messages are projected directly onto the curved membranous surface using mobile laser beamers that can rotate 320 degrees. HoloPro (transparent projection) surfaces suspended in the clouds serve as an additional image medium.

Unter den Wolken, auf der Produktebene, verbindet der „Weg der Lösungen" drei jeweils radial angeordnete Präsentationsbereiche mit eigenen Farbcodes (abgestimmt auf die Wolken). Der einheitlich anthrazitfarbene Bodenbelag ist im hinteren Bereich des Messestandes zu einer 7 m hohen Welle aufgebogen, die die Infrastruktur verbirgt.

Beneath the clouds, at product level, the "path of solutions" connects the three radially arranged presentation areas with their own colour codes (matching the clouds). In the rear area of the trade fair stand the uniformly anthracite-coloured floor covering is bent upward to form a 7-metre-high wave that conceals the infrastructure.

Auf der Erdgeschoss-
ebene hat jeder Prä-
sentationsbereich eine
eigene Farbkennung.

On ground-floor level
each presentation area
has its own colour
scheme.

Der „Weg der Lösungen" verbindet unter dem in den Wolken verborgenen „Pfad der Sinne" die drei Präsentationsbereiche.

The "path of solutions" connects the three presentation areas beneath the "pathway of the senses" up amongst the clouds.

Year	**2002**
Location	**Hanover**
Trade Fair	**Hanover Messe Industry**
Exhibitor	**Siemens AG Automation & Drives, Nuremberg**
Architect	**Zeeh Bahls & Partner Design GmbH, Dießen: Mr. Bahls, Mr. Strauß Luxoom-Mediendesign, Berlin: Mr. Sauerwein, Mr. Trojahn**
Lighting	**Luxoom-Mediendesign, Berlin**
Size	**3,000 m²**
Realisation	**Zeeh Design Messebau GmbH, Puchheim designafairs exhibition services, Erlangen**
Graphics / Communication	**Publicis Kommunikationsagentur, Erlangen: Mr. Haubold**
Photos	**Industriefoto Koerber: Herr Koerber Fotopolis Alexander Busch, Weimar**

Würfelspiel aus Kartons
Cardboard Cubes

D'Art Design Gruppe für VDP –
Verband deutscher Papierfabriken,
HPV, PTS, Verband pro Karton

D'Art Design Group for VDP –
German Paper Manufacturers' Association,
HPV, PTS, Pro Carton Association

Der VDP (Verband Deutscher Papierfabriken), der Hauptverband der Papier, Pappe und Kunststoff verarbeitenden Industrie (HPV), die papiertechnische Stiftung (PTS) und der Verband Pro Carton stellten der weiterverarbeitenden Industrie die Produktvorteile der Materialien Papier, Karton und Pappe als Verpackungsmaterial vor. Es sollte neugierig gemacht werden auf die Vielzahl der Möglichkeiten von Papier, den kreativen Umgang mit Material, die Vielfalt und Dynamik von Verpackungslösungen.

Drei PC-Terminals in Form von aufgefalteten Pappschachteln dienen als Informationsquelle für die Angebote der beteiligten Organisationen und Mitgliedsunternehmen. Ein Besuchermagnet ist die raumgreifende Skulptur aus unzähligen weißen Kartons, die unter der Decke zu schweben scheinen und quasi eine im Wind bewegte Baumkrone bilden.

The German Paper Manufacturers' Association (VDP), Leading Association for Paper, Cardboard and Plastics Processing Industries (HPV), Paper Technology Foundation (PTS), and the Pro Carton Association presented the product advantages of paper, card and cardboard as packaging materials to the processing industry. The aim was to arouse curiosity about the wealth of possibilities of paper, the creative use of materials, and the variety and dynamism of packaging solutions.

Three PC terminals in the form of unfolded cardboard boxes serve as information sources for the products of the participating organisations and member companies. A magnet for the visitors is the imposing sculpture constructed of numerous white cardboard boxes that appear to be floating beneath the ceiling creating a virtual treetop swaying in the wind.

An der weißen Rück-
wand ergibt sich ein
spannendes Spiel aus
den bewegten Schat-
ten des Kartonmobiles.

The moving shadows
of the cardboard
box mobile create a
dramatic effect on
the white rear wall.

papier, karton, pappe – die alleskönner

Year	**2002**
Location	**Duesseldorf**
Trade Fair	**Interpack**
Exhibitor	**VDP – Verband deutscher Papierfabriken e.V.**
Architect	**D'Art Design Gruppe, Neuss: Karin Blanke, Jochen Höffler, Dominik Hof**
Size	**100 m²**
Realisation	**ACES GmbH, Neuss**
Photos	**Karin Unterstenhöfer-Müller, Duesseldorf**

Projektionskubus
Projection Cube

Christian Werner Industrial Design /
do.designoffice
für Otto Entsorgungssysteme

Christian Werner Industrial Design
and do.designoffice
for Otto Entsorgungssysteme

Die sehr geschlossene Außenform des Standes erklärt sich aus dem Hauptmerkmal des Entwurfs: dem inneren Projektionsraum. Dessen acht Projektionsflächen werden gebildet von vier gleichförmigen Wandwinkeln, bespannt mit einer Gaze, die vom Boden abgesetzt ist, so dass die Wände zu schweben scheinen. Die Winkel stehen mit Abstand zueinander auf einer quadratischen Grundfläche, die Zwischenräume bilden die Eingänge ins Standinnere. Im Zentrum befindet sich eine transparente Infotheke, in den vier Ecken stehen auf Podesten die Exponate.

Die umlaufenden Projektionen sind unterschiedliche, miteinander kommunizierende Filmsequenzen. Eine Mischung aus Grafik und Produktinformation wird ergänzt durch Szenen zum Thema Müll und Entsorgung im öffentlichen Raum, die unerwartet geschnitten sind und eher einem Roadmovie ähneln. Die Produkte sind branchenunüblich inszeniert und ästhetisiert.

The very closed external form of the stand can be explained by the main design feature: the internal projection area. Its eight projection surfaces are formed from four identically shaped corner wall elements covered with a screen that is raised from the ground giving these elements a floating appearance. The corners are positioned together, some distance apart, on a square base; the spaces created in between form the entrances to the stand's interior. In the centre is a transparent info stand; the exhibits are arranged on platforms in the four corners.

The rotating projections are varied film sequences that communicate with each other. A mixture of graphics and product information is supplemented by scenes relating to waste and waste management in the public domain, which are unexpectedly cut and are more reminiscent of a road movie. The products are stage-managed and aestheticised in a manner untypical for the industry.

Besprechungsräume, Bistro und Küche sind außerhalb des eigentlichen Präsentationsbereichs angegliedert.

The meeting areas, bistro and kitchen are all positioned outside of the actual presentation area.

Schnitt

Section

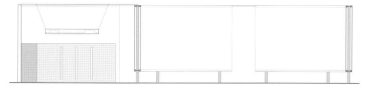

Grundriss

Plan

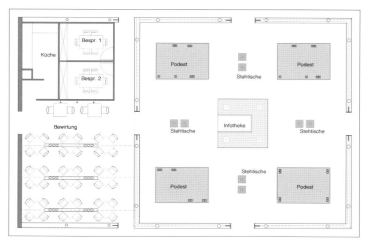

Nur spärliche und un-
gewöhnliche Einblicke
werden dem Messe-
besucher bei der An-
näherung an den Stand
ermöglicht.

The visitors are afforded
only scanty, unusual
views as they approach
the stand.

Year	**2002**
Location	**Munich**
Trade Fair	**IFAT 2002**
Exhibitor	**Otto Entsorgungssysteme GmbH & Co. KG, Kreuztal**
Architect	**Christian Werner Industrial Design, Hollenstedt / Appel: Christian Werner do.designoffice, Pulheim: Grischa Göddertz**
Lighting	**iGuzzini, Ligne Roset**
Size	**294 m²**
Realisation	**Viva Messebau, Hanover**
Graphics / Communication	**AK Media, Aachen**
Photos	**Wolfgang Pulver, Munich**

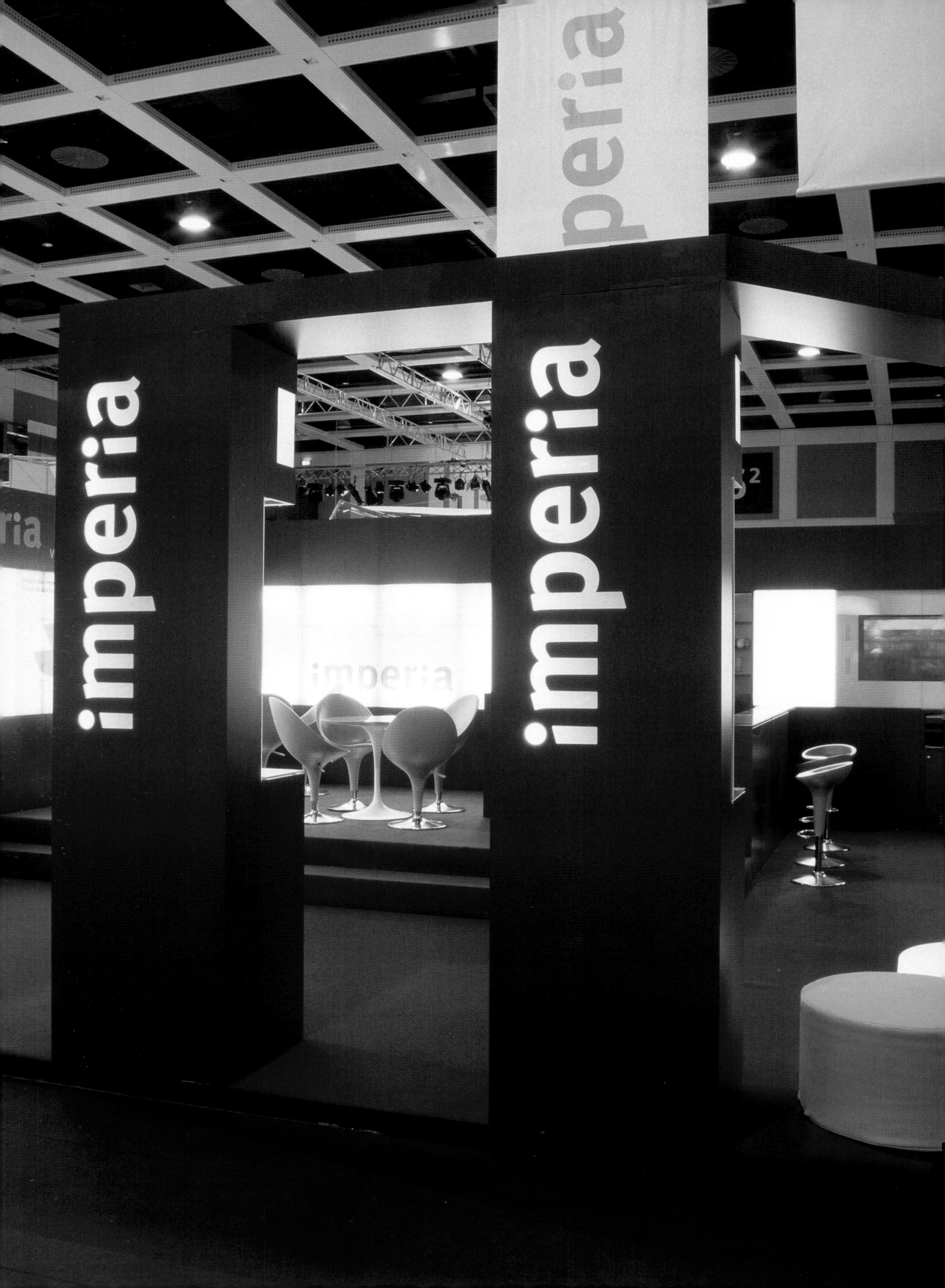
imperia
imperia
imperia

Ochsenblutrote Module

Oxblood-Red Modules

B-DREI
für Imperia

B-DREI
for Imperia

Der Software-Hersteller Imperia wollte sich mit einem farbigen, atmosphärischen, modularen Systemstand von seinen Mitbewerbern absetzen.

Auf einem niedrigen Podest befinden sich möbelähnliche Körper: Wandelemente und frei stehende Präsentationselemente, die untereinander durch horizontal darüber gelegte Verbindungsträger zusammengefasst sind und so den Stand räumlich nach oben abschließen. Die Wandelemente funktionieren mit hinterleuchteten Plexiglastafeln und davor angebrachter Grafik auch als Display, die Präsentationselemente beinhalten die Technik zur Vorführung von Software bzw. realisierten Projekten. Der Computer befindet sich in einem abschließbaren Schrankelement im unteren Teil, die Tastatur auf einem ausziehbaren Tastatureinschub. Der Flachbildschirm ist in eine Plexiglastafel bündig eingebaut, so dass die horizontale Fläche auch als Ablagefläche zu benutzen ist.

The software producer Imperia wanted to stand out from its competitors with a coloured, atmospheric, modular system stand.

Bodies resembling furniture are positioned on a low platform: wall elements and free-standing presentation elements are combined by overhead, horizontal cross beams that demarcate the top of the stand spatially. The wall elements, with their backlit Plexiglas plates and graphics displayed in front, also serve as a display; the presentation elements house the technical equipment used to present the software and realised projects. The computer is located in the lower part of a lockable cupboard element, the keyboard on a pullout keyboard tray, and the flat-screen is fitted flush into a Plexiglas plate so that the horizontal surface can also be used to put things on.

Vor den Wänden, die durch aneinandergereihte Wandelemente im Wechsel mit Präsentationselementen gebildet werden, können Prospekthalter aus Plexiglas angebracht werden.

Plexiglass holders for brochures can be fixed in front of the walls, which are formed by strung together wall elements alternating with presentation elements.

Year	**2002**
Location	**Berlin**
Trade Fair	**Internet World**
Exhibitor	**Imperia AG, Hürth**
Architect	**B-DREI, Stuttgart:** **Astrid Kurz, Jürgen Voss** **with: Martin Grether**
Lighting	**Concept: B-DREI, Stuttgart**
Size	**64 m²**
Realisation	**AMS Ausstellungs Miet Stand GmbH** **Joinery: Türen Mann**
Graphics / Communication	**B-DREI, Stuttgart: Sabine Linde** **with: Martin Grether**
Photos	**Isabell Simon**

Niedrig und hoch

High and Low

Leitner GmbH
für Durst

Leitner GmbH
for Durst

Der Inselstand der Durst Phototechnik AG teilt sich in einen doppelstöckigen und einen einstöckigen Standbereich – beide erstellt mit dem System L10 Doppelstock der Leitner GmbH.

Der hohe Bereich wirkt nach außen sehr ruhig durch den mit Jalousien schlicht verkleideten Doppelstock im Mittelteil des Standes und die hohen, mit hellem Textil bespannten Winkelelemente, die nur mit dem Firmennamen bedruckt sind und die im Innern den Hintergrund für kleine Besprechungsbereiche bilden.

Der einstöckige Bereich dagegen, der durch die strahlende Lichtdecke dominiert wird, zeigt sich auch nach außen expressiver: Grafik und Großbilder sind auf die teils durchsichtigen, teils transluzenten und teils geschlossenen Systemelemente aufgebracht.

Durst Phototechnik AG's island stand is divided into a double-storey and a single-storey stand area – both created using the L10 double-storey system by Leitner GmbH.

The high area has a very calm external appearance. This can be attributed to the simple effect of the venetian blinds covering the double storey in the centre of the stand and to the high angular elements with overstretched light fabric that are simply printed with the company name and form the backdrop to small meeting areas in the interior.

The single-storey area, on the other hand, which is dominated by the radiant light ceiling, has a more expressive external appearance. The graphics and blow-ups are displayed on the partly transparent, partly translucent and partly closed system elements.

Einstöckiger (oben)
und doppelstöckiger
Standbereich (links).

Single-storey (top) and
double-storey stand
area (left).

Year	**2002**
Location	**Cologne**
Trade Fair	**Photokina**
Exhibitor	**Durst Phototechnik AG, Brixen (I)**
Architect	**Leitner GmbH, Waiblingen** **with: Designer Societät Stuttgart**
Lighting	**System lighting L10,** **System lighting L22: Special model** **with daylight quality**
Size	**480 m²**
Realisation	**Leitner GmbH, Waiblingen:** **Leitner Services GmbH**
Graphics / Communication	**Designer Societät Stuttgart** **with: Peter Horlacher**
Photos	**Frank Erber, Ostfildern**

Let's share
VARIETY

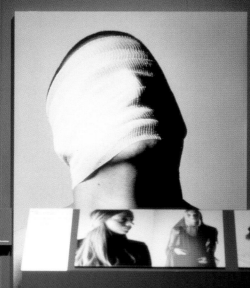

Farbkorridor
Colour Corridor

Atelier Brückner
für Kodak

Atelier Brückner
for Kodak

Unter dem Motto „Share Moments, Share Life" entstand in einer kompletten Messehalle ein Bühnenraum, dessen gestaffelte Portale über einen langen, sich weitenden und verengenden, geschwungenen Korridor die beiden Zugänge zur Halle verbinden und den Raum gliedern.

Rechts und links des Korridors schließen sich die Ausstellungsbereiche der einzelnen Geschäftsfelder von Kodak an, die vom Besucher problemlos als Szenen erkannt werden, weil sich auch dieses Mal wieder eine auffällige, farbige Gestaltung über Wände und Böden zieht und gute Orientierung bietet.

Under the motto "Share Moments, Share Life" a stage area was created in a complete exhibition hall, its oblique portals connecting the two entrances to the hall with a long, widening and narrowing, curved corridor that divides the area.

The exhibition areas of the individual business fields of Kodak adjoin the corridor to the right and left. These are essentially easily recognized by the visitor as sets because here also a striking, colourful arrangement is again used that extends over walls and floors and aids orientation.

Jeder Ausstellungs-
bereich der einzelnen
Geschäftsfelder mit
seiner eigenen Farb-
gebung zeigt auf un-
terschiedlichen Trägern
die Bandbreite der
Bilddarstellung.

Each exhibition area of
the individual business
fields has its own
colouring and demon-
strates the range of
image representation
using various media.

Einzelne überdimensionale Leuchtkästen und übergroße Figuren
sorgen als Bildsilhouette in den unterschiedlichen Räumen für
Aufmerksamkeit. Durch das Spiel mit den Proportionen ver-
ändert sich das Verhältnis zwischen Raum und Besucher, so dass
die Besucher die Welt der Bilder real zu betreten scheinen. Diese
wird gebildet durch die „Gerahmten Blicke" entlang des Korridors und die farblich unterschiedenen „Guckkastenbühnen"
rechts und links des breiten Hauptweges, deren Einzelräume
eigene Bildwelten entwickeln. Sie zeigen auf unterschiedlichen
Trägern die Bandbreite der Bilddarstellung.

The silhouetted images created by individual enormous light
boxes and oversized figures in the different areas capture the
visitor's attention. This play on proportions alters the relation-
ship between space and the visitor in such a way that the
world of images actually appears to be accessible by the visitor.
This is fashioned by the "framed views" along the corridor and
the different-coloured "gogglebox stages" to the right and
left of the wide main walkway, whose individual areas show
their own worlds of images. Using different mediums they
demonstrate the range of image representation.

Auch die Möblierung
unterstützt das Spiel
der Geschichten von
Farben und Erlebnissen.

The furnishings also
contribute to the play of
colours and experiences.

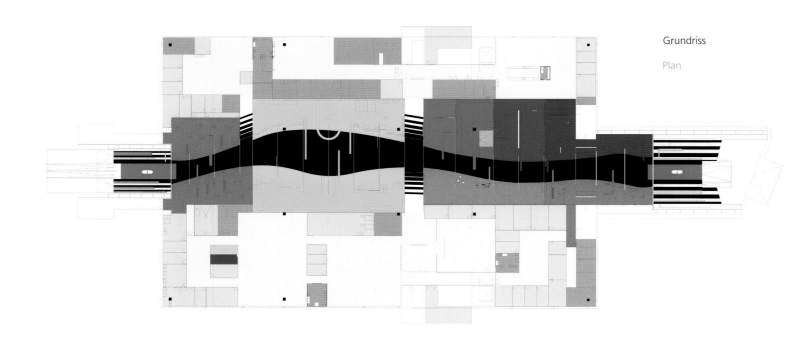

Grundriss

Plan

Vom geschwungenen
Hauptweg mit den
großen Bildportalen
zweigen die einzelnen
Präsentationsräume ab.

The individual presen-
tation areas branch off
from the curved main
pathway with the large
image portals.

Year	**2002**
Location	**Cologne**
Trade Fair	**Photokina**
Exhibitor	**Kodak GmbH, Stuttgart**
Architect	**Atelier Brückner, Stuttgart:** **Project Architect: Dominik Hegemann** **Team: Sayman Bostanci, Gesa Dörfler,** **Lars Jürgens, Britta Nagel,** **Anja Neuefeind, Dirk Schubert**
Lighting	**Realisation: Bluepool AG, Hanover**
Size	**8,600 m^2**
Realisation	**Bluepool AG, Hanover**
Graphics / Communication	**Atelier Brückner, Stuttgart:** **Project: Birgit Kölz** **Team: Catherine François,** **Marianna Messina, Florian Widman** **Realisation: Heinze + Malzacher GmbH,** **Stuttgart**
Photos	**Dieter Leistner, Würzburg** **Kodak GmbH, Stuttgart**

Systemfreiheit
Freedom through the System

Team Burkhardt Leitner
constructiv GmbH & Co. /
colour concept mann
für Burkhardt Leitner constructiv

Team Burkhardt Leitner
constructiv GmbH & Co. /
colour concept mann
for Burkhardt Leitner constructiv

Ausgehend von den beiden Basissystemen constructiv PILA und CLIC zeigt Burkhardt Leitner constructiv unter dem Thema „office in emotion" die Weiterentwicklung und Vertiefung der Produktpalette für die Geschäftsbereiche Office, Display und Messe. Es werden aber nicht nur neue technische und architektonische Detaillösungen präsentiert, sondern auch innovative Arbeits-, Material- und Farbwelten erschlossen. Beispielhafte Baukörper, die gleichzeitig ausgestelltes Produkt und Messesystem sind – die MeetingBox, die MiniOfficeBoxen als Ein-Personen-Zellenbüros und die RecreationBox –, zeigen auf der Messe die Strukturierung und Flexibilisierung von Großraumbüros mittels personalisierter und individuell ausgestatteter, optisch wie akustisch geschützter Arbeitsplätze.

Taking the two basic systems constructiv PILA and CLIC as a starting point, Burkhardt Leitner constructiv presents under the "office in emotion" theme the development and extension of its product range for the three business sectors office, display and trade fair. In addition to the presentation of new technical and architectonic detailed solutions, innovative worlds of work, material and colour are also developed. Exemplary structures – the meeting box, the mini office boxes as one-person office booths and the recreation box – are both exhibits and a trade fair system at the same time. They show at the trade fair the structuring and flexibility of open-plan offices by means of personalised and individually furnished workspaces that are optically and acoustically shielded.

Wände und Tür der
RecreationBox sind aus
bielastischen Stoffen
und wölben sich nach
außen.

The walls and door of
the recreation box are
made of flexible
materials and curve
outwards.

Year	**2002**
Location	**Cologne**
Trade Fair	**Orgatec**
Exhibitor	**Burkhardt Leitner constructiv GmbH & Co., Stuttgart**
Architect	**Burkhardt Leitner constructiv GmbH & Co., Stuttgart Colour Concept: colour concept mann, Nürtingen: Brigitte Mann**
Lighting	**Burkhardt Leitner constructiv GmbH & Co., Stuttgart with: LFF, Solingen**
Size	**96 m²**
Graphics / Communication	**Fleischmann + Kirsch, Stuttgart**
Photos	**Lothar Bertrams, Stuttgart**

Rasterplan

Grid System

Stefan Zwicky
für Denz

Stefan Zwicky
for Denz

Anstatt mit einer konventionellen Produktpräsentation von Büromöbeln wird das Produkt D3 by Denz als Kunstinstallation präsentiert. An der Rückwand des schwarzen Standes, der aus einem Podest, einer Rück- und Seitenwand besteht, finden sich die drei Architektonischen Begriffe von Vitruvius: firmitas, utilitas, venustas. Dieser verbale, zweidimensionale Eingriff sollte als kurzes Pamphlet an der Wand Erstaunen und Irritation auslösen. Davor findet sich in rasterartiger Aufreihung auf einer möglichst großen Fläche das Produkt D3 by Denz, das auf eine Würfelform von 80 x 80 x 80 cm reduziert wurde.

Instead of a conventional product presentation of office furniture, the D3 by Denz product is presented as an art installation. On the back wall of the black stand, which comprises of a platform plus a rear and side wall, are the three architectonic concepts of Vitruvius: firmitas, utilitas, venustas. This verbal two-dimensional display, in the form of a short lampoon on the wall, is meant to provoke astonishment and irritation. The D3 by Denz product, which has been reduced onto a cube measuring 80 x 80 x 80 cm, is lined up in a grid-like formation in front of the lampoon on as large an area as possible.

Diese dreidimensionale installationsartige Maßnahme verbild-
licht Ordnung, Kompetenz und Größe. Ein Spiegel auf einer
kleinen Seitenwand vergrößert den Raum noch weiter und
trennt den Hauptteil von einem Beratungsbereich mit Sitz-
gelegenheit und Verpflegung ab.

This three-dimensional installation-like measure illustrates order,
competence and size. A mirror on a small side wall increases
the perspective still further and divides the main part from a
meeting area with seating and refreshments.

Die Grundstruktur mit dem ebenfalls schwarzen Linoleumboden bildet eine Black Box in Anlehnung an die bestehende Corporate Identity von Denz.

The black skeletal structure and linoleum floor form a black box, making reference to Denz's existing Corporate Identity.

Year	**2002**
Location	**Cologne**
Trade Fair	**Orgatec**
Exhibitor	**Denz & Co., Nänikon (CH)**
Architect	**Stefan Zwicky, Zurich (CH)**
Lighting	**Spot lighting**
Size	**5 x 23.5 m**
Realisation	**Denz & Co., Nänikon (CH)**
Graphics / Communication	**Stefan Zwicky, Zurich (CH) with: Büro 4, Zurich (CH)**
Photos	**Oliver Schuster, Stuttgart**

Schwungvoll
Comfort Curves

design hoch drei
für Interstuhl Büromöbel

design hoch drei
for Interstuhl Büromöbel

Eine langgestreckte Ellipse aus gebogenen, farbigen Decken-bannern bestimmt den rechteckigen Messestand, der mit leicht transparentem Stoff raumhoch nach außen abgeschlossen ist. Von den Gängen aus wird zwar Einblick gewährt, innen jedoch findet sich ein ruhiger Hintergrund für die Präsentation des Büromöbelherstellers Interstuhl mit den verschiedenen Produkt-schwerpunkten und Marken.

Die Deckenbanner in kräftigen Farben analog zur Corporate Identity des Unternehmens dienen der Orientierung im Raum und integrieren die umfangreichen Produktinformationen. Ein auf dem hellen, unbehandelten Holzboden auflackierter Rundweg führt den Besucher durch die Ausstellung. Die Produkte selbst stehen entweder direkt auf dem Boden oder auf schlichten, kubischen Podesten.

A long ellipse of curved coloured ceiling banners characterises the rectangular trade fair stand, which is closed on the outside with lightly transparent material reaching to the top of the hall. Although it is possible to see into the stand from the corridors, the interior presents a calm background for the presentation of the office furniture manufacturer Interstuhl, with the various product highlights and brands.

The ceiling banners in strong colours analogous to the company's corporate identity aid orientation within the space and integrate the extensive product information. A path var-nished onto a light untreated wooden floor guides the visitor through the exhibition. The products themselves are positioned either directly on the floor or on simple cubic platforms.

Die Besprechungs- und Nebenräume begrenzen den Stand
nach hinten; auf den geschlossenen, lichtgrauen Wandflächen
werden wichtige Ergonomiethemen grafisch und mit Texten
erläutert.

The meeting and adjoining areas demarcate the back of
the stand; important ergonomic themes are explained using
graphics and texts on the closed, light-grey wall surfaces.

Skizze

Sketch

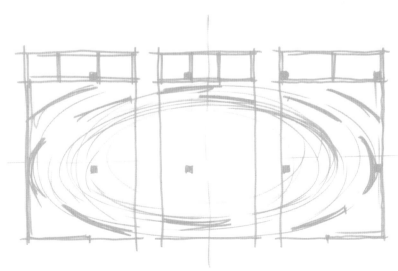

Elegant und klar
werden über die Gra-
fik Informationen
vermittelt.

The graphics convey
information elegantly
and clearly.

Year	**2002**
Location	**Cologne**
Trade Fair	**Orgatec**
Exhibitor	**Interstuhl Büromöbel GmbH + Co. KG, Meßstetten**
Architect	**Svantje Miras, Stuttgart**
Lighting	**Light & Magic, Hohenheim**
Size	**about 1000 m²**
Realisation	**Raumtechnik Messebau GmbH, Ostfildern**
Graphics / Communication	**Design: design hoch drei GmbH + Co. KG, Stuttgart: Project Management, CD: Susanne Wacker, AD: Diethard Keppler, Graphic Design: Regina Müller**
Photos	**Engelhardt + Sellin, Aschau i. Ch. Lithography: Reprofessional, Stuttgart**

Klare Raumstrukturen
Clear Spatial Structures

f/p Design
für Mabeg

f/p Design
for Mabeg

Der Stand erlaubt viele Ein- und Durchblicke. Die klar geglie-
derte Plattform ist dreigeteilt und wird im mittleren Drittel
durch einen auffällig orangefarbenen, runden Empfangstresen
bestimmt. Zu beiden Seiten befinden sich die Produktpräsen-
tationen: auf der einen Seite eine zweigeschossige bühnenartige
Raumstruktur, die im unteren Bereich die Programme für
„Arbeiten und Konferieren" sowie „Empfangen und Warten"
zeigt. Im Obergeschoss verbirgt sie Lounge und Konferenzraum
hinter halbtransparenten Glaswänden mit markanten Edel-
stahlstreben oder orangefarbenen, leuchtenden Glaswänden.
Auf der anderen Seite wird die Präsentation in und mit den
neuen Produktprogrammen gebildet.
    Getreu der Idee, kreative Synergien zu finden und zu fördern,
gibt es zwei Gäste auf dem Stand: die Schweizer Unternehmen
Revox sowie WOGG.

The stand's construction allows the visitor to look through and
into it from various angles. The clearly structured platform is
divided into three parts and is characterised in the middle third
by a striking, round, orange reception desk. At either side are
the product presentations: on the one side a two-storey stage-
like spatial structure showing the "work and conference" and
"reception and waiting" programs on the lower level. On the
upper level the structure conceals the lounge and conference
room behind semitransparent glass walls with prominent stainless-steel struts or bright, orange-coloured glass walls. On the
other side is the presentation in and with the new product
programs.
    True to the idea of finding and encouraging creative synergies,
there are two guests on the stand: the Swiss companies Revox
and WOGG.

Zurückgezogen und
dennoch mit Ausblick
können im Ober-
geschoss Gespräche
geführt werden.

Meetings with a
view can be held in
the secluded upper
storey.

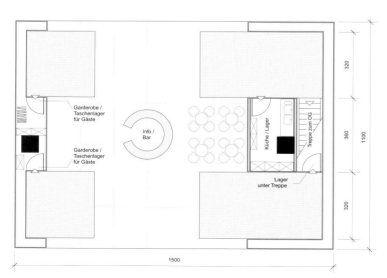

Grundriss

Plan

Zusätzlich zu den
bereits vorhandenen
werden sechs neue
Programme präsen-
tiert.

In addition to the
programmes already
available, six new ones
are presented.

Year	**2002**
Location	**Cologne**
Trade Fair	**Orgatec 2002**
Exhibitor	**Mabeg, Soest**
Architect	**f / p design gmbh, Frankfurt a. M.: Fritz Frenkler, Anette Ponholzer**
Size	**200 m²**
Realisation	**Mabeg, Soest**
Graphics / Communication	**Büro Blank Communication Services**
Photos	**Thomas Mayer, Neuss**

Leuchtende Zelte

Glowing Tents

Joachim Sparenberg,
Sedus Stoll AG und
Paul Wilke, La Senzo
für Sedus Stoll

Joachim Sparenberg,
Sedus Stoll AG and
Paul Wilke, La Senzo
for Sedus Stoll

Nähert sich der Besucher dem Messestand der Sedus Stoll AG, leuchten ihm aus dem umgebenden Dunkel die Bauteile wie Martinslaternen entgegen.

5,5 m hohe, frei hängende oder stehende Stahlkonstruktionen unterschiedlicher Durchmesser, die mit buntem Lycra bespannt sind, wecken aber auch Assoziationen zu den Behausungen der Nomadenvölker: den Iglus der Eskimos, den Jurten der Mongolen oder Wigwams der Indianer. Laut Sedus Stoll führte tatsächlich die Beschäftigung damit zu dieser einprägsamen, aber dennoch sehr abstrakten und vieles offen lassenden Form, die Ort der inneren Welt der Ruhe, der Konzentration auf das Thema und Ort der Begegnung (mit dem Kunden) ist. Elf dieser in kürzester Zeit auf- und abbaubaren Hüllen, die als System für weitere Messen gedacht sind, bergen neun neue Produktfamilien und zwei Serienprodukte.

On approaching the trade fair stand of Sedus Stoll AG, the components shine out at the visitor like paper lanterns in the surrounding darkness.

5.5-metre-high suspended or freestanding steel constructions of differing diameters, which are covered in brightly coloured lycra, conjure up associations with nomadic dwellings: the igloos of the Eskimos, the yurts of the Mongolians or the wigwams of the Indians. According to Sedus Stoll, its preoccupation with the latter led to this striking yet very abstract form that leaves much open to the imagination and represents a place of inner calm, of concentration on the theme and also a place to meet (with the client). Eleven of these structures, which can be assembled and dismantled in no time at all and are intended as a system for further trade fairs, hold nine new product families and two series products.

Kreisrunder Bodenbelag – aus einem Material, ohne Höhenwechsel – definiert die Präsentationsfläche für die Exponate, die im Innern durch je 20 vertikal gereihte Kaltneonröhren neutral tageslichtbeleuchtet sind und die übergroßen Lampions nach außen stark bunt leuchten lassen.

A perfectly circular floor covering – using a different material but with no height difference – defines the presentation area for the exhibits. The latter are illuminated in the interior by 20 vertically hung cold cathode fluorescent tubes that simulate neutral daylight; on the outside the oversized Chinese lanterns shine brightly in contrast.

Year	**2002**
Location	**Cologne**
Trade Fair	**Orgatec**
Exhibitor	**Sedus Stoll AG, Waldshut**
Architect	**Concept: Joachim Sparenberg, Sedus Stoll AG** **Design: Paul Wilke, La Senzo**
Lighting	**Design: Arne Christian Brandes**
Size	**650 m²**
Realisation	**Hypsos, Soesterberg (NL)**
Graphics / Communication	**Sedus Stoll AG**
Photos	**Reinhard Schwederski, Detmold**

Zweigeteilt
Split in Two

colour concept mann
für Wüst

colour concept mann
for Wüst

Die Wüst GmbH produziert und vertreibt qualitativ hochwertige Tufting-Teppichböden für den anspruchsvollen Wohn- und Objektbereich. Als übergreifendes Grundelement für die Positionierung des Unternehmens, für die Produktgestaltung, die Präsentation und die Kommunikation gilt die Farbe als konzeptioneller Ansatz. Deswegen ist die „Botschaft Farbe" das Hauptmerkmal dieses kleinen Messestandes.

Der Stand ist vertikal geteilt in die zwei Corporate-Identity-Farben der Firma: im linken Teil in der hellen CI-Farbe werden die Produkte fürs Wohnen präsentiert, im rechten Teil in der dunklen CI-Farbe die Produkte fürs Büro. Der sägeraue, gebrochen weiß lasierte Holz-Bretterboden bildet einen wohltuenden Kontrast zum Textilen der präsentierten Produkte. Lediglich um die quadratische Sitzbankinsel in der Mitte des Standes liegt Teppichboden, dort aber nur, um die Präsentationsmöglichkeiten zu erweitern (Teppichbodenmuster, Teppichbodenrollen mit Banderole, Musterkarten in Schubladenschränken etc.).

Wüst GmbH produces and sells high-quality tufted carpeting for superior living and business space. Colour, which forms the basic concept, is the all-encompassing fundamental element for the corporate positioning as well as for the product design, presentation and communication. For this reason the "colour message" is the main feature of this small trade fair stand.

The stand is vertically divided into the company's two CI colours: the products for the home are presented in the left part in the light CI colour; the products for the office are presented in the right part in the dark CI colour. The rough sawn, broken-white finished floorboards contrast agreeably with the textiles of the products on display. Carpeting is laid only around the square island of benches in the centre of the stand with the sole purpose, however, of expanding the possibilities of product presentation (carpet samples, rolls of carpet with banderoles, sample cards in drawer files etc.).

Über den gezielten Einsatz von Licht wird die Visualisierung von Farbe, Struktur, Textur, Oberfläche und Materialität unterstützt. Der Stand selbst ist vom Hallenlicht beleuchtet. Neben der Farbe ist der Einsatz des Quadrats als Gestaltungselement auffällig: vom Logo über die Formate der Printmedien bis zu den Möbeln und den Details zieht es sich konsequent durch.

The selective use of light aids visualisation of colour, structure, texture, surface and materials. The stand itself is illuminated by the hall light. Apart from the use of colour, the use of the square as a design feature is also striking: it crops up consistently, in the logo, the formats of the printed media as well as in the furniture and the details.

Grundriss

Plan

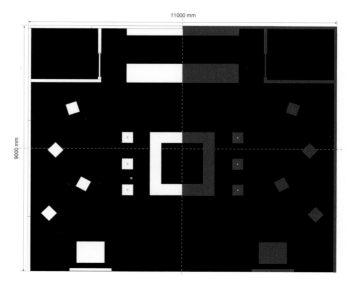

Auch innerhalb der
Regale sind die
Produktmuster nach
Farbgruppen geordnet.

The product samples
are even sorted
according to colour
group within the
shelves themselves.

Year	**2002**
Location	**Cologne**
Trade Fair	**Orgatec**
Exhibitor	**Wüst GmbH & Co. / maltzahn group of companies, Kempen**
Architect	**colour concept mann, Nürtingen: Brigitte Mann Wüst GmbH & Co., Kempen: Gerhard Hoffe**
Size	**99 m²**
Realisation	**Reinhold Backmann GmbH, Senden**
Graphics / Communication	**Concept and design: colour concept mann, Nürtingen: Brigitte Mann Realisation: Realwerk G. Lachenmaier GmbH & Co. KG, Reutlingen / MK Hoffe Marketing und Kommunikation, Schmallenberg**
Photos	**Lothar Bertrams, Stuttgart**

Rot sehen

Seeing Red

Beate Steil
für capricorn development

Beate Steil
for capricorn development

Auf diesem auffällig roten Messestand präsentiert sich die Firma capricorn development anlässlich der Vermarktung ihres mäanderförmigen Bauprojekts capricorn Haus im Düsseldorfer MedienHafen.

Seit Mitte der 80er-Jahre widmen sich capricorn (heute capricorn engineering) der Restauration und Wartung alter Rennfahrzeuge, später entstand capricorn automotive (Prototypen und Vorserien für die Automobilindustrie), und bei capricorn development werden seit neuestem intelligente Konzepte für moderne Gebäude erdacht, die sich durch richtungsweisende Technik auszeichnen.

The presentation of the company capricorn development on this prominent red trade fair stand marks the occasion of the marketing of its meandering building project capricorn house in the Duesseldorf Media Docks.

Since the mid 1980s capricorn (today capricorn engineering) has devoted itself to the restoration and maintenance of old racing cars; capricorn automotive was founded later (prototypes and pilot production for the automobile industry), and more recently capricorn development has been involved in thinking up intelligent concepts for modern buildings, whose outstanding feature is their trend-setting technology.

In einer Hülle aus einem filigranen System mit roten textilen Wänden und weißen textilen Deckenflächen bestimmt die prägnante Form eines mäanderförmigen Körpers die Stand-fläche. Er ist bestückt mit vier Monitoren, auf denen ein Multi-mediavideo Stadtlage, Architekturidee, technische Lösungen und die Projektpartner in einer collagenhaften Umsetzung zeigt.

The concise form of a meandering body defines the area of the stand within an exterior created from a filigree system with red textile walls and white textile ceiling areas. It is equipped with four monitors on which a multimedia video presents a collage of information including the location, architectural idea, technical solutions and project partners.

Der mäanderförmige
Körper dient auch als
halbhohe Abtrennung
bei Besprechungen auf
den kissenbestückten
Sitzwürfeln dahinter.

The meandering body
also serves as a low
dividing element when
meetings are being
held on the cushioned
seating cubes behind it.

Year	**2002**
Location	**Munich**
Trade Fair	**Expo Real**
Exhibitor	**capricorn development, Mönchengladbach**
Architect	**Concept and Design: Beate Steil, Duesseldorf** **Concept: Sibylle Schwarz, Stuttgart**
Lighting	**Klartext Messebau, Krefeld (Erco System)**
Size	**36 m²**
Realisation	**Klartext Messebau, Krefeld**
Graphics / Communication	**Klartext Messebau, Krefeld** **Concept and Realisation Multimedia** **Video: CHBP, Cologne** **Leporello postcard, Concept Multimedia** **Video: Beate Steil**
Photos	**Klartext Messebau, Krefeld**

Spannende Bänder

Strip Tension

Martin Birrer
für Büro Fürrer Office Design

Martin Birrer
for Büro Fürrer Office Design

Jedes zweite Jahr präsentieren am Designers' Saturday in Langenthal (CH) Firmen aus dem Schweizer In- und nahen Ausland an den Produktionsstandorten verschiedener Unternehmen ihre Produkte. 2002 stand der Designers' Saturday unter dem Thema „Begegnungen mit dem Unerwarteten". Die Firma Büro Fürrer stellte in einer großen Halle der Firma Glaströsch aus. In seiner Präsentation befasst sich der Hersteller klar gestalteter und eher kühler Bürosysteme mit dem persönlichen Bereich des einzelnen Mitarbeiters.

Entlang der Innenseite des Ausstellungskubus sind zusätzlich noch Bilder ausgestellt: Details von persönlichen Arbeitstischen. Die Installation wird zu einem räumlichen und inhaltlichen Begegnungsort, an welchem die Eigenart des Unternehmens auf spielerische Weise dargestellt wird.

At the Designers' Saturday held every two years in Langenthal, Switzerland, companies from Switzerland and its surrounding countries present their products at the production sites of various firms. In 2002 the theme of the Designers' Saturday was "Brushes with the unexpected". The company Büro Fürrer exhibited in a large hall belonging to the company Glaströsch. The manufacturer of clearly designed and somewhat stark office systems bases its presentation on the personal space of individual employees.

In addition, pictures are exhibited along the inside of the exhibition cube: details of personal desk space. The installation is transformed into a meeting place, spatially and in terms of content, in which the individuality of the company is presented in a playful manner.

Im Zentrum der Installation – einer Struktur aus hängenden Stahlrahmen, die mit Kunststoffbändern umwickelt sind – hängt auf einer Höhe von drei Metern ein Drucker, der fortlaufend Wünsche der Mitarbeiter ausdruckt. Die Blätter fallen aus dem Drucker zu Boden, der Besucher wird neugierig und beginnt zu lesen.

In the centre of the installation – a structure constructed of suspended steel frames bound with plastic strips – hanging at a height of three metres is a printer printing out employees' wishes non-stop. The printed sheets fall out of the printer onto the floor; the visitor becomes curious and starts to read them.

Der rot bespannte
Stahlrahmen des Aus-
stellungskubus, der
wenige Zentimeter
vom Boden abgeho-
ben ist, leuchtet in der
Halle von weitem.

The red-covered steel
frame of the exhibition
cube, which is raised a
few centimetres from
the ground, can be
seen shining in the hall
from afar.

Year	**2002**
Location	**Langenthal (CH)**
Trade Fair	**9. Designers' Saturday**
Exhibitor	**Büro Fürrer Office Design, Zurich (CH)**
Architect	**Concept und Architecture:** **Martin Birrer, Bern (CH)** **with: Alexandra Schäfer, Büro Fürrer,** **Zurich (CH)**
Size	**50 m²**
Realisation	**Stahlblau Martin Blaser, Bern (CH)**
Photos	**Martin Birrer, Bern (CH)**

Bürobauernhof
Farmhouse Office

Stefan Zwicky
für Denz

Stefan Zwicky
for Denz

Mit einer alle Besucher zum Lächeln animierenden Installation reagiert die Denz AG auf den Ort ihrer Produkteschau am Designers' Saturday. Im Erdgeschoss eines großen Bauernhauses in unmittelbarer Nachbarschaft des Design Center Langenthal empfängt die Belegschaft der Denz AG (inkl. Inhaber und Geschäftsführer) unter dem Motto „Denz's kleine Tierschau" den Besucher in Appenzeller Trachten.

Die Bauern sind die Mitarbeiter/Berater, die Tiere die Produkte. Kühe und Schweine sind aus Versatzteilen des Erfolgsmodells D3 by Denz und weiteren Büroaccessoires collagenartig zusammengebaut. So sollen der Unterhaltungswert erhöht und die Begegnungen am Designers' Saturday gefördert werden. Dem ländlichen Thema entsprechend wird der Gast in einer Art „Besenbeiz" bewirtet und mit einem Appenzeller Hackbrettduo musikalisch unterhalten. Zur professionellen Information dienen zwei große Prospektregale mit Referenzunterlagen des Produkts.

Denz AG's reaction to the location of their product show at the Designers' Saturday is an installation that provokes smiles from all the visitors. The staff of Denz AG (including the owner and MD), attired in local Appenzeller traditional dress, receives the visitors on the ground floor of a large farmhouse in the vicinity of the Langenthal Design Centre under the motto "Denz's little animal show".

The farmers are the employees/consultants and the animals are the products. Cows and pigs are put together like a collage from set pieces from the D3 by Denz successful model and other office accessories. The amusement factor is thereby increased and meetings at the Designers' Saturday encouraged. In accordance with the rural theme, the guest is entertained in a kind of traditional pub with musical accompaniment by a local Appenzeller dulcimer duo. Two large shelves of brochures containing product references provide professional information.

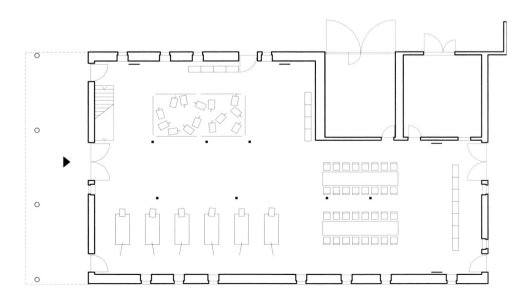

Grundriss

Plan

Year	**2002**
Location	**Langenthal (CH)**
Trade Fair	**9. Designers' Saturday**
Exhibitor	**Denz & Co., Nänikon (CH)**
Architect	**Stefan Zwicky, Zurich (CH)**
Size	**290 m²**
Realisation	**Denz & Co., Nänikon (CH)**
	Stefan Zwicky, Zurich (CH)
Graphics / Communication	**Denz & Co., Nänikon (CH)**
Photos	**Exhibition: Heinz Unger, Zurich (CH)**
	Portrait: Urs Walder, Zurich (CH)

Designers' Saturday, Langenthal

Lichtregal
Light Shelf

Licht + Raum AG / Room by Wellis AG
Eigenstand

Licht + Raum AG / Room by Wellis AG
Own Stand

Room by Wellis und Licht + Raum realisierten auch 2002 wieder einen gemeinsamen Auftritt in den Lager- und Kellerräumen des Gebäudes von Création Baumann, der eine sehr direkte Reaktion auf den Ort und die Qualität des Raumes, aber auch das Resultat kontinuierlicher Auseinandersetzung im gemeinsamen Arbeitsprozess ist.

Auf einem Podest durchschneidet ein 60 m langes, mit zahlreichen Leuchten ausgestattetes Regalsystem, das Kurt Erni für Wellis entworfen hat, den langen Gang. Die sinnliche Wirkung der farbigen Reflexionen steht bewusst im Gegensatz zur hellen Härte und Gradlinigkeit der stringenten Installation. Das emotionale Licht eröffnet aber ebenso sensibel die Diskussion mit der schroffen Kargheit des rohen Kellerraums.

The year 2002 saw a joint appearance by Room by Wellis and Licht + Raum in the storage and cellar areas of the Création Baumann building. This appearance represents not only the very direct reaction to the location and to the quality of the space, but is also the result of continual disagreement in the joint work process.

A platform supports a 60m-long shelving system fitted with numerous lights – designed by Kurt Erni for Wellis – which cuts the long corridor in two. The sensorial effect of the colourful reflections intentionally contrasts with the light angularity and severity of the stringent installation. The emotional quality of the light, however, initiates with equal sensitivity a conflict with the rough sparseness of the austere cellar space.

Je nach Blickrichtung erscheint das beleuchtete Regalsystem von Kurt Erni farbig bzw. farblos.

Depending on the viewing angle, the illuminated shelve system by Kurt Erni appears either coloured or colourless.

Ausstellung einiger Produkte von Room by Wellis AG auf unterleuchteten Podesten vor einer Wand des Spulenlagers.

An exhibition of selected products by Room by Wellis AG on platforms lit from below in front of one of the walls of the coil storage area.

Mit entsprechender
Beleuchtung wird ein
Palettenstapel zum
Ausstellungsobjekt.

With the appropriate
lighting, a stack of
pallets is transformed
into an exhibit.

Seitenansicht

Side elevation

Grundriss

Plan

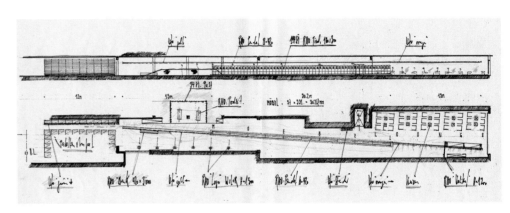

Year	**2002**
Location	**Langenthal (CH)**
Trade Fair	**9. Designers' Saturday**
Exhibitor	**Licht + Raum AG, Ittigen (CH) + Room by Wellis AG, Willisau (CH)**
Architect	**Beat Kaufmann, Licht + Raum AG, Ittigen (CH) Kurt Erni, Room by Wellis AG, Willisau (CH)**
Lighting	**Licht + Raum AG, Ittigen (CH)**
Realisation	**Licht + Raum AG, Ittigen (CH) + Room by Wellis AG, Willisau (CH)**
Graphics / Communication	**Licht + Raum AG, Ittigen (CH) + Room by Wellis AG, Willisau (CH)**

VARTA PoLiFlex®

VARTA PoLiFlex
PLF 423568

3.7 V,
780 mAh

Streifenkraft
Power Stripes

häfelinger + wagner design
für Varta Microbattery

häfelinger + wagner design
for Varta Microbattery

Der Eckstand mit seinem schmalen, langen Grundriss ist in Kabinenbereiche an beiden Enden und einen offenen Präsentationsbereich in der Mitte aufgeteilt. Varta Microbattery ist ein neu entstandener Unternehmensbereich. Die Produktpalette umfasst Batterien für mobile High-Tech-Produkte und viele industrielle Anwendungen. Ein schmales, umlaufendes Band, das ein wichtiges Element des Corporate Design ist, bildet als beleuchtetes Fenster die Präsentationsvitrine der Produkte. Fast alle Wände, die analog zur Titelgestaltung der Broschüren in der Tiefe in mehreren Ebenen farbig gegliedert sind, sind Träger von Image- und Produktkommunikation.

The corner stand with its long, narrow ground plan is divided into cubicles at either end and an open presentation area in the middle. Varta Microbattery is a newly developed company sector. The product range includes batteries for mobile high-tech products and various applications in industry. A narrow circulating band in the shape of an illuminated window, which is an important element of the corporate design, forms the product showcases. Almost all of the walls, which are divided lower down into several strata of colour analogous to the title design of the brochures, are vehicles for conveying image and product communications.

In die Wand, die mit
zwei Pendeltüren den
Besprechungsbereich
abtrennt, ist ein
Plasmabildschirm ein-
gelassen; etwas aus
der Mitte der Front
herausgerückt befin-
det sich ein HoloPro-
Screen.

A plasma screen is
built into the wall that
sections off the meet-
ing area with its two
swing doors; at the
front of the stand,
more or less in the
middle, is a protruding
HoloPro screen.

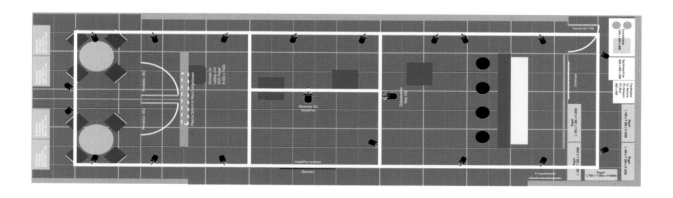

Grundriss

Plan

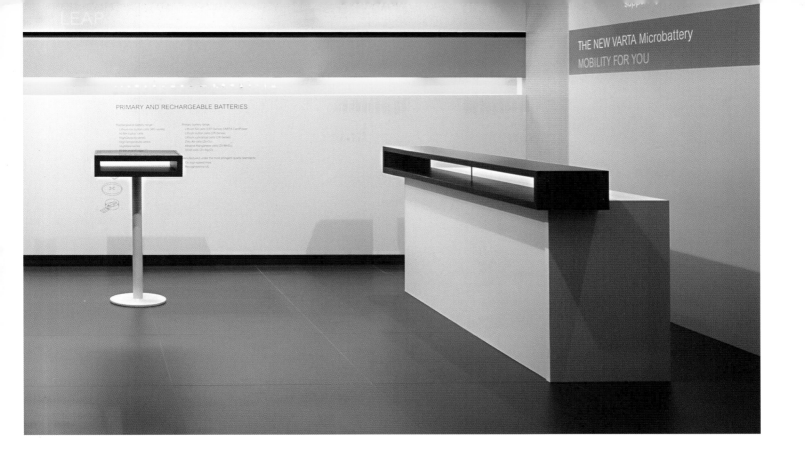

Year	**2002**
Location	**Munich**
Trade Fair	**Electronica**
Exhibitor	**Varta Microbattery GmbH, Ellwangen**
Architect	**häfelinger + wagner design, Munich: Thomas Häussler, Frank Wagner**
Lighting	**dergrünefisch, Munich: Elke Gutjahr**
Size	**63 m²**
Realisation	**dergrünefisch, Munich: Elke Gutjahr Schreinerei Jacoby, Starnberg**
Graphics / Communication	**häfelinger + wagner design, Munich**
Photos	**Michael Heinrich, Munich**

Aufgewölbt

Upward Curves

schindlerarchitekten
für Armstrong / DLW

schindlerarchitekten
for Armstrong / DLW

In einer dreidimensionalen Raumskulptur werden die üblicherweise zweidimensionalen Bodenbeläge präsentiert. Von der horizontalen Bodenfläche sind verschiedene Bahnen zur Rückwand bis zu 4,5 m aufgebogen. In diese Bahnen, die nicht aus Bodenbelag bestehen, sind die Bodenmuster in Form intarsienartiger Streifen an wenigen ausgesuchten Stellen eingelassen.

Die verschiedenen Produktsegmente Office, Retail, Education, Health Care und Hospitality (Hotel und Gastronomie) sind auf jeweils einer Bahn mit zwei Belägen in unterschiedlichen Rhythmen vertreten. Diese Exponate wurden nach rein ästhetischen Gesichtspunkten ausgewählt. Nur an einer Stelle des Standes, auf der Ebene des Catering-Bereichs, ist ein neuer Bodenbelag großflächiger verlegt.

The generally two-dimensional floor coverings are presented in a three-dimensional spatial sculpture. Various lanes curve upwards to a height of 4.5 metres onto the rear wall from the horizontal floor surface. The floor patterns are set into these lanes, which are not made of floor covering, in the form of inlaid strips in a few selected spots.

The various product segments, – office, retail, education, health care and hospitality (hotel and gastronomy) – are each represented in varying rhythms on a different lane with two floor coverings. These exhibits are selected from a purely aesthetic point of view. A new floor covering has been more extensively laid at only one point on the stand, that is, on the level of the catering area.

Grafik und Lichtprojektionen, die inhaltlich das Thema Bodenbelag aufnehmen, ergänzen die Inszenierung; es gibt keine
Trennung von Architektur und Kommunikation.

Graphics and light projections, which take up the theme
of floor covering, complete the setting; there is no division of
architecture and communication.

Year	**2003**
Location	**Munich**
Trade Fair	**Bau 03**
Exhibitor	**Armstrong / DLW AG**
Architect	**schindlerarchitekten, Stuttgart: Uwe Schindler Project Management: Christine Witte Design: Olga Skaba with: Büro für Gestaltung, Kommunikation und Kultur, Aalen: Ine Ilg**
Lighting	**TLD Planungsgruppe GmbH, Wendlingen: Jochen Brauns**
Size	**about 150 m²**
Realisation	**Messeprojekt Leipzig GmbH, Leipzig Graphics: Fa. Stadelmaier, Kirchheim Lighting and Projection: Neumann und Müller Veranstaltungstechnik GmbH, Wendlingen**
Graphics / Communication	**Büro für Gestaltung, Kommunikation und Kultur, Aalen: Ine Ilg**
Photos	**Peter Bauer, Aalen**

Profilierte Welle
Contoured Wave

a.ml Architekturwerkstatt und
Oliver Schuster Visuelle Gestaltung
für Holzbau Seufert-Niklaus

a.ml Architectural Studio and
Oliver Schuster Visuelle Gestaltung
for Holzbau Seufert-Niklaus

Der kompakte Messestand, der nach drei Seiten geschlossen ist, wird von einem einfarbig weißen Profil geprägt, das nach vorne durch eine raumhohe Glaswand und nach hinten von einer Holzrückwand mit Fotos abgeschlossen ist. Das Profil zieht sich vom fast geraden Boden über eine stark gewellte Querwand zu einer leicht geschwungenen Decke. Es ist an der Wand so geformt, dass es als Sitzmöbel dienen kann und zum Verweilen einlädt.

The compact trade fair stand, closed on three sides, is characterised by a uniformly white profile that is closed at the front by a ceiling-high glass wall and at the rear by a wooden back wall bearing photos. The profile extends from the virtually level floor over a highly corrugated short wall to a slightly curved ceiling. It is formed against the wall in such a way that it can serve as seating, tempting the visitor to rest a while.

Im Innern wird das räumliche Gefüge durch die zwei präsentierten Fensterelemente und eine Theke aus schwarzem Glas gegliedert.

On the inside the two presented window elements and a black-glass bar divide the spatial structure.

Year	**2003**
Location	**Munich**
Trade Fair	**Bau 03**
Exhibitor	**Seufert-Niklaus GmbH, Bastheim**
Architect	**a.ml + partner, Nuremberg:** **Prof. Matthias Loebermann, Eric Alles** **Oliver Schuster Visuelle Gestaltung,** **Stuttgart**
Size	**30 m²**
Realisation	**Seufert-Niklaus GmbH, Bastheim**
Graphics / Communication	**Oliver Schuster Visuelle Gestaltung,** **Stuttgart**
Photos	**Oliver Schuster Visuelle Gestaltung,** **Stuttgart**

Konstruktive Plastik
Constructive Sculpture

büro hartmannich
für Anton Heggenstaller und Lignatur

büro hartmannich
for Anton Heggenstaller and Lignatur

Auf kleiner Grundfläche sollten die Möglichkeiten der Produkte von Lignatur dargestellt und mit einem auffälligen Stand visuell unmittelbar verdeutlicht werden. Lignatur entwickelt innovative Hohlkonstruktionen aus Holz. Die Firma Anton Heggenstaller ist ein deutscher Holzproduzent, der an diesen Holzbauelementen beteiligt ist. Die produzierten Flächen- und Kastenelemente sind in den unterschiedlichsten Querschnitten erhältlich und zeichnen sich durch geringes Gewicht bei hoher Stabilität aus. Diese Eigenschaften der Bauelemente werden durch die Höhe des doppelstöckigen Standes von 8 m und durch darin frei schwebende Stege verdeutlicht.

The possibilities offered by Lignatur's products are demonstrated on a small surface area and visually presented with a striking stand. Lignatur develops innovative hollow wooden constructions. The company Anton Heggenstaller is a German wood producer involved in the construction of these wooden elements. The surface and case elements are available in a variety of cross-sections and their remarkable feature is that they are highly stable despite their light weight. The 8-metre-high two-storey stand and the freely suspended bridges within it demonstrate this feature of the construction elements.

In einem grafischen, dreidimensionalen Spiel mit horizontalen und vertikalen Linien und Flächen aus den Lignatur-Elementen, die für den Stand Wände und Ebenen bilden, entstehen immer neue überraschende Bilder.

Surprising new images are constantly being created in a graphic three-dimensional game with horizontal and vertical lines and surfaces from the Lignatur elements, which form the stand's walls and planes.

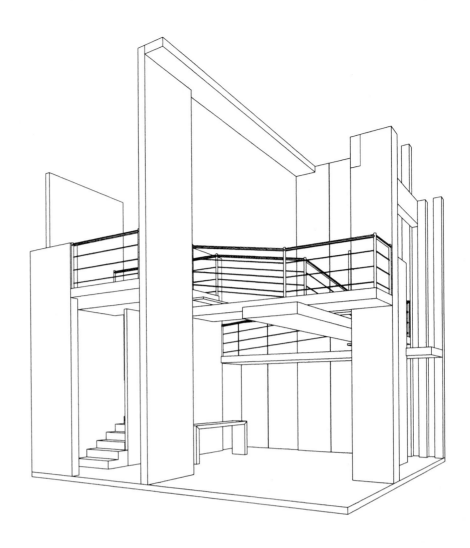

Year	**2003**
Location	**Basle (CH)**
Trade Fair	**Swissbau**
Exhibitor	**Anton Heggenstaller AG, Unterbernbach Lignatur AG, Waldstatt (CH)**
Architect	**büro hartmannich, Munich: Dipl.-Ing. (FH) Andrea Hartmann, Dipl.-Ing. (FH) Achim Mannich**
Lighting	**büro hartmannich**
Size	**42 m²**
Realisation	**Schreinerei Paul Färber, Wolferstadt**
Graphics / Communication	**Hans Neudecker, Leutkirch (for Anton Heggenstaller AG) level-east, St. Margrethen (CH) (for Lignatur AG)**
Photos	**Foto Studio Heuser, Munich Dipl.-Ing. (FH) Andrea Hartmann**

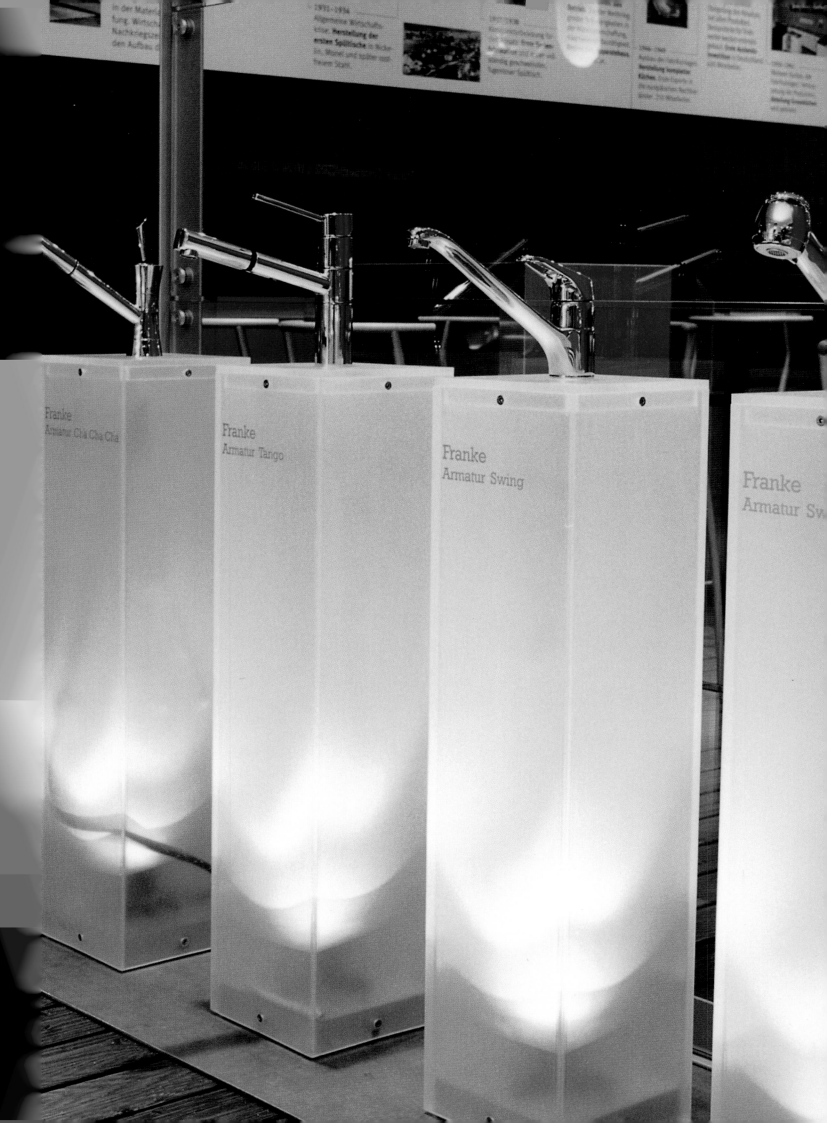

Spülenparade
Sink Parade

Zeeh Design Karlsruhe
für Franke Küchentechnik

Zeeh Design Karlsruhe
for Franke Küchentechnik

Wie eine Terrasse aus Holzdielen scheint der Messestand des weltmarktführenden Spülenherstellers über dem Wasser zu schweben. An Glasscheiben, die vor dem Geländer der Terrasse befestigt sind, rieselt das Wasser herab und läuft dann in ein Becken.

Auf der dunklen Bodenfläche kommen die hellen Exponate gut zur Geltung. Diese sind neu entwickelte, leicht zu bestückende Spülendisplays aus geschliffenem, hinterleuchtetem Plexiglas. Von dieser wie vereist wirkenden Fläche heben sich die verschiedenen Spülen-Oberflächen und -Farben ab, gleichzeitig wird aber die Masse an Exponaten auch in ein ruhiges und gleichmäßiges Erscheinungsbild eingebunden.

The trade fair stand of the world market leader in sink-unit manufacture appears to be suspended above the water like wooden decking. The water trickles down glass panes, which are secured in front of the railings of the decking, before flowing into a pool.

The dark floor surface shows the light-coloured exhibits to their best advantage. The latter are newly developed, easy-to-fit sink-unit displays made of polished backlit Plexiglas. The various sink-unit surfaces and colours stand out against the frozen effect of this surface: at the same time the mass of exhibits is also integrated in a calm, composed image.

Die rote Wand, Teil der
CI von Franke, schirmt
den Loungebereich ab
und hebt die Demon-
strationsspüle hervor.

The red wall, part of
Franke's CI, shields the
lounge area and ac-
centuates the demon-
stration sink units.

Grundriss

Plan

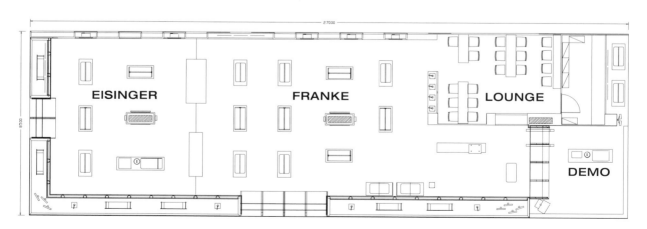

Zusätzlich zum Auftritt von Franke musste die Premium-Marke Eisinger als eigenständiger Bereich eingebunden werden. Um das Grundkonzept beizubehalten, den Bereich aber dennoch von Franke abzusetzen, wurde der Hell-Dunkel-Kontrast hier umgedreht.

In addition to Franke's appearance, the premium brand Eisinger had to be included as an independent area. In order to retain the basic concept, but at the same time set the two areas apart, the light–dark contrast was reversed in Franke's area.

Drei große Decken-segel grenzen den Stand zur Hallendecke ab und binden die Hallensäulen ein.

Three large ceiling canvases separate the top of the stand from the hall ceiling and integrate the supports.

Der Stand ist modular
aufgebaut, der Dielen-
boden wurde als Sys-
tem konzipiert, und
auch die neu ent-
wickelten Spülen-
displays erfüllen den
Anspruch an leichte
Transportierbarkeit.

The stand is designed
as a modular system,
the woodstrip flooring
was conceived as a
system, and even the
newly developed sink-
unit displays fulfill the
requirement of being
easily transportable.

Franke Compact CPX 651, weltweit über 1,2 Mio. mal verkauft.

Eines der Edelstahl-
Exponate ist in die
Bodenfläche eingelas-
sen.

One of the stainless-
steel exhibits is em-
bedded in the floor
area.

Year	**2003**
Location	**Basle (CH)**
Trade Fair	**Swissbau**
Exhibitor	**Franke Küchentechnik AG, Aarburg (CH)**
Architect	**Zeeh Design Messebau GmbH Karlsruhe: Design: Björn Dette Architecture and Project Management: Rolf Ratz, Joachim Schaupp, Alexander Vojinovic**
Lighting	**Zeeh Design Karlsruhe**
Size	**Head stand 27 x 8.5 m**
Realisation	**Zeeh Design Karlsruhe**
Graphics / Communication	**Franke Küchentechnik AG, Aarburg (CH): Project Management: Nicolas Christen**
Photos	**Jörg Müller, Aarau (CH) ghr-visuell GmbH: Frank Reiser**

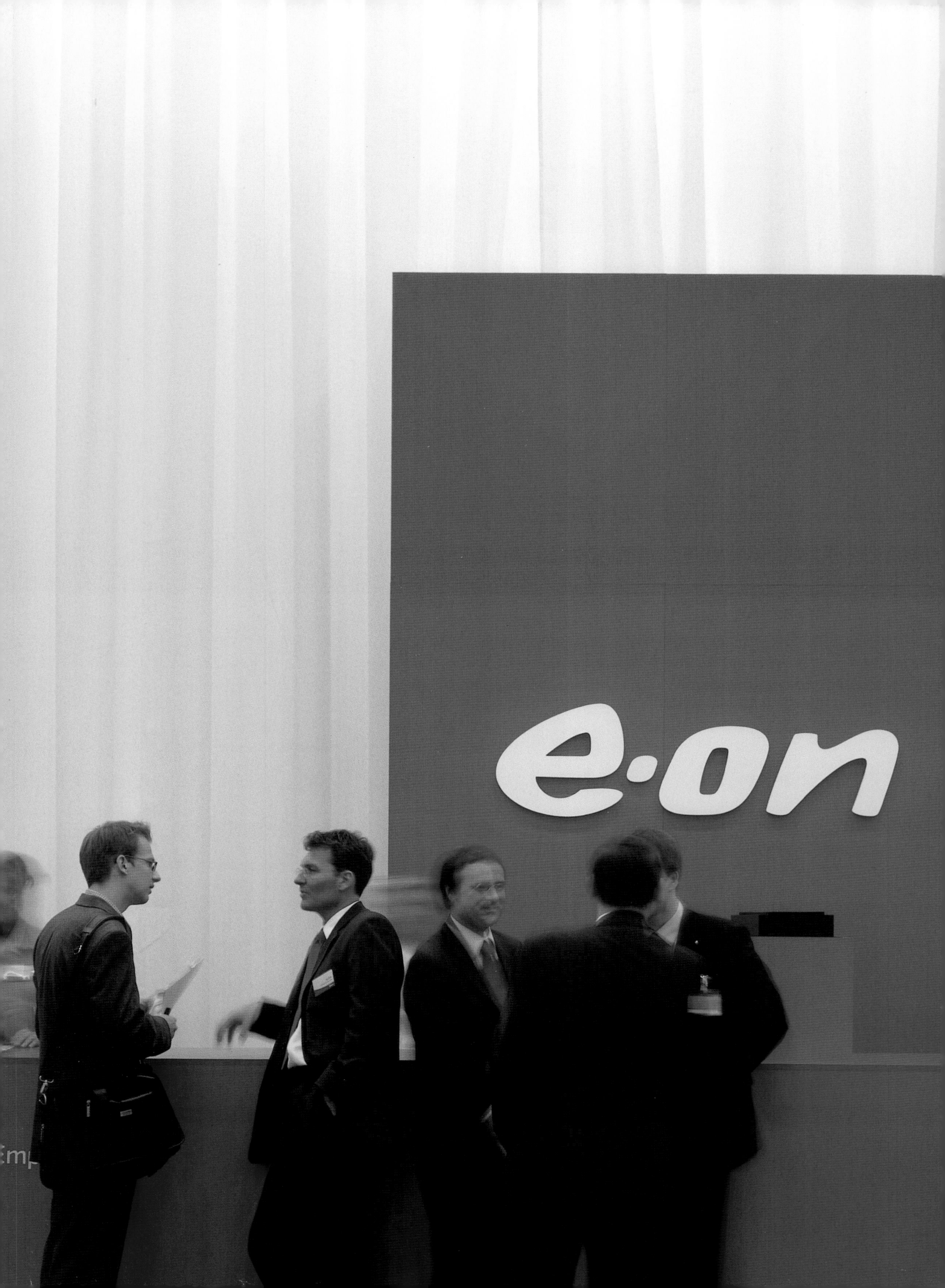
e·on

In the Box

In the Box

avcommunication GmbH
für E.ON Sales & Trading

avcommunication GmbH
for E.ON Sales & Trading

E.ON Sales & Trading ist der Vertriebs- und Handelszweig der E.ON AG, deswegen umschließt eine weithin sichtbare E.ON-rote Klammer schützend einen daraus weiß hervorleuchtenden Kern, die E.ON Sales & Trading Welt. Die weißen Stoffbahnen des leuchtenden Stoffkubus im Innern überragen die rote Klammer um 1,5 m. Im Innenbereich, der nur von ausgewählten Besuchern betreten werden kann, herrscht Weiß vor. Das E.ON-Rot markiert als Akzent die Service-Bausteine: Trolleys, Service-Wagen zur Bedienung und vor allem die roten Schachteln der Giveaways, die wie ein Minimal-Art-Kunstwerk eine ganze Wand dominieren.

E.ON Sales & Trading is a sales and marketing subsidiary of E.ON. For this reason an E.ON-red bracket, visible from afar, protectively encompasses a white core shining out from within it, the E.ON Sales & Trading world. The white lengths of fabric that make up the bright fabric cube in the interior tower 1.5 metres above the red bracket. White is the predominant colour in the interior, which only selected visitors are allowed to enter. The E.ON red accentuates the service elements: serving trolleys and, above all, the small red boxes of the give-aways that dominate an entire wall like a piece of minimal art.

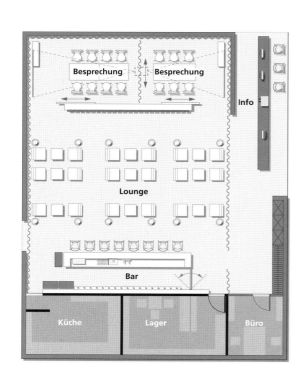

Grundriss

Plan

Rote, eigens gefertigte
Turnschuhe sind der
Inhalt der in strengem
Raster angebrachten
Giveaway-Schachteln.

The giveaway boxes
displayed in a strict
grid-like formation
contain self-manufac-
tured red gym shoes.

Durch die abgehängten Deckensegel wirkt die Lounge trotz des 6,5 m hohen Innenraums sehr intim.

The suspended ceiling canvas gives the lounge a very intimate feel despite its 6.5 metre high interior.

Year	**2003**
Location	**Essen**
Trade Fair	**E-world of Energy**
Exhibitor	**E.ON Sales & Trading, Munich**
Communication Concept / Architecture	**avcommunication GmbH, Ludwigsburg: Norbert W. Daldrop, Andreas Olbrich, Günter Rein, Adrian von Starck**
Lighting	**avcommunication GmbH, Ludwigsburg Bluepool AG, Leinfelden-Echterdingen**
Size	**200 m²**
Realisation	**Bluepool AG, Leinfelden-Echterdingen**
Graphics	**avcommunication GmbH, Ludwigsburg**
Photos	**Roland Halbe, Stuttgart**

Beschleunigungsspuren
Fast Lanes

Schmidhuber + Partner
für Audi

Schmidhuber + Partner
for Audi

Das Markenimage von Audi wird verstärkt in Richtung Sport-
lichkeit ausgebaut. Für diese Neuorientierung steht der Begriff
des „Spurwechsels" aus dem automobilen Sprachgebrauch,
der Assoziationen von Beschleunigung hervorruft.

Eine dunkle Bodenfläche ist durch eingelegte Stahl-Lisenen
in zahlreiche Spuren aufgegliedert, denen die Positionierung
der Serienfahrzeuge folgt. Durchkreuzt wird das System von
diagonal angeordneten Inszenierungsspuren, die sich auch
noch durch Material und Farbe von der restlichen Fläche abheben: eine medial bespielte „Zeitspur" hebt und überschlägt
sich über eine andere, um nach vollzogenem Spurwechsel
parallel weiterzulaufen. Ein Loop dient als architektonischer
Rahmen für das Messe-Highlight und versinnbildlicht zugleich
als Superzeichen den „Spurwechsel".

The sportive aspect of Audi's brand image is greatly reinforced.
The term "changing lanes", from motoring usage, stands for this
new orientation and conjures up associations with acceleration.

A dark floor surface is divided into various lanes by inlayed
steel pilaster strips, which the positioning of the production
vehicles follows. Diagonally arranged lanes, whose material
and colour also stand out from the rest of the surface, cross
over this system: a "time lane" in the middle rises and crosses
over another in order to continue running parallel with it after
changing lanes. A loop serves as an architectonic frame for the
trade fair highlight and symbolises at the same time "changing
lanes".

Auch die weitere Stand-
architektur nimmt
diese Formensprache
auf: das bereits bei
anderen Ständen ein-
gesetzte Lounge-
Gebäude mit einer
selbstleuchtenden
Membran-Fassade wird
durch ein gerundetes
Ende des Baukörpers
dynamisiert.

The rest of the stand's
architecture picks up
on this use of forms:
the lounge building
with a self-illuminating
membranous façade,
which has already been
used for other stands,
is given a dynamic ap-
pearance by a rounded
end to the structure.

Die Stellung der
Serienfahrzeuge folgt
streng den eingelegten
Spuren auf dem Holz-
boden; die Inszenie-
rungsspuren und der
Loop durchkreuzen
dieses System.

The positioning of the
production vehicles
adheres strictly to the
inlaid lanes on the
wooden floor; the
staging lanes and the
loop cross over this
system.

Year	**2003**
Location	**Geneva (CH)**
Trade Fair	**International Motor Show**
Exhibitor	**AUDI AG, Ingolstadt**
Architect	**Schmidhuber + Partner, Munich: Kerstin Arleth, Doris Eizenhammer, Nicole Hohmann, Andreas Kienle, Jürgen Paul, Susanne Schmidhuber, Jens Vorbröcker, Martin Weber**
Lighting	**Four to one: Scale Design, Hürth**
Size	**2,450 m² ground floor 650 m² first floor**
Realisation	**Ernst F. Ambrosius & Sohn GmbH, Frankfurt a. M.**
Graphics / Communication	**Totems Communications BV, Amsterdam (NL) / Stuttgart**
Photos	**Andreas Keller, Altdorf**

Geformte Bänder
Formed bands

Bürling Architekten mit KMS
für DaimlerChrysler

Bürling Architects with KMS
for DaimlerChrysler

Der ganze Stand wird von schmalen, parallelen Bändern be-stimmt, die vor- und zurückspringen. Im mehrgeschossigen Bereich vor der Hallenrückwand haben sie durch die Addition als Ansichtsflächen eine starke, einheitliche Fernwirkung, die noch dadurch verstärkt wird, dass es sich um 6 m hohe, geätzte Glasscheiben vor LEDs handelt, die zeitweise reflektieren, dann aber wieder die integrierten Präsentationsflächen des hoch leistungsfähigen, räumlichen, grafischen Trägerelements zeigen.

Die Bänder werden zu Bodenbelag, Sitzbänken, Theken (Info-theke, Prospekttheke, Accessoirestheke), Wänden, räumlichen Leitfunktionen, Dachlandschaften. Es entwickelt sich aus und mit ihnen darauf, davor, dahinter, darin, darunter, dazwischen.

The entire stand is defined by narrow, parallel bands, some in the foreground, others in the background. In the multi-storey area in front of the rear wall of the hall, their combined appearance has a powerful uniform effect when viewed from a distance; this effect is intensified by the 6-metre-high etched sheets of glass, positioned in front of LEDs, that at times reflect and at others show the integrated presentation surfaces of the highly efficient, spatial graphics display.

The bands turn into floor covering, benches, counters (in-formation counter, brochure counter, accessories counter), walls, spatial guides, and roof landscapes. The presentation area is produced from and with the bands, above, in front of, behind, within, below, between.

Im offenen, zentralen Bereich finden die Weltpremiere des CLK-Cabrios und die Präsentation der E-Klasse statt, im hinteren mehrgeschossigen Teil ist auf der höheren Ebene der AMG-Bereich. Der Besucher bewegt sich hier durch die Bänder. Er hat Ein- und Ausblicke, die von oben auch immer wieder in den unteren Bereich und über den gesamten Messestand reichen. Die Oberfläche der Bänder, die in warme Holzflächen eingebettet sind, besteht aus seidenmatt glänzendem Aluminium bzw. Glas.

The world premier of the CLK convertible and the presentation of the E-class take place in the open central area. The AMG area is situated on the higher level in the rear multi-storey part. Here the visitors move through the bands. From above they can see into and onto the stand, with views every now and again of the lower area and over the whole trade fair stand.
The bands, which are embedded in warm wooden surfaces, - have a gleaming satin-finish aluminium or glass surface.

Year	**2003**
Location	**Geneva (CH)**
Trade Fair	**International Motor Show**
Exhibitor	**DaimlerChrysler AG, Stuttgart / Mercedes-Benz**
Complete Organisation	**DaimlerChrysler AG, Dept. MKP / B**
Architect	**Bürling Architekten, Stuttgart**
Concept and Communication	**KMS, Munich**
Graphics	**Firma Schüttenberg, Duesseldorf**
Lighting	**Design: TLD-Lichttechnik, Wendlingen** **Realisation: Sound + Light, Leonberg**
Size	**about 2,950 m²**
Realisation	**Ernst F. Ambrosius & Sohn GmbH, Frankfurt a. M.**
Media	**Planning: Light & Magic, Hohenstein** **Realisation: ETF Event Engineering n.v., Wavre (B)**
Media Design and Film Production	**gate 11, Munich**
Sound	**Realisation: Neumann + Müller, Wendlingen**
Photos	**Andreas Keller, Altdorf**

Stilvoller Auftritt
Stylish Appearance

Kauffmann Theilig & Partner
für Maybach

Kauffmann Theilig & Partner
for Maybach

Der Messestand der Marke Maybach ist Teil des DaimlerChrysler Auftritts, der sich aus der Konzerndarstellung (DaimlerChrysler Corporated), Mercedes-Benz, smart, Chrysler und Maybach zusammensetzt. Souverän, in stilvoller Eleganz präsentiert sich die Marke Maybach innerhalb des Gesamtauftritts aller DaimlerChrysler Marken.

Die klare, minimalistische Formensprache der Architektur und der reduzierte Einsatz von Kommunikationsmedien unterstützen die imposante Wirkung des Produktes.

The Maybach brand's trade fair stand is part of the Daimler-Chrysler appearance made up of the group representation (DaimlerChrysler Corporated), Mercedes-Benz, smart, Chrysler and Maybach. Sovereign and with a stylish elegance the brand presents Maybach within the overall appearance of all DaimlerChrysler brands.

The clear, minimalist form language of the architecture and reduced use of communications media supports the impressive effect of the product.

Les grandes visions débutent souvent par une petite illumination.
Jede grosse Vision beginnt mit einer kleinen Erleuchtung.

MAYBACH 62

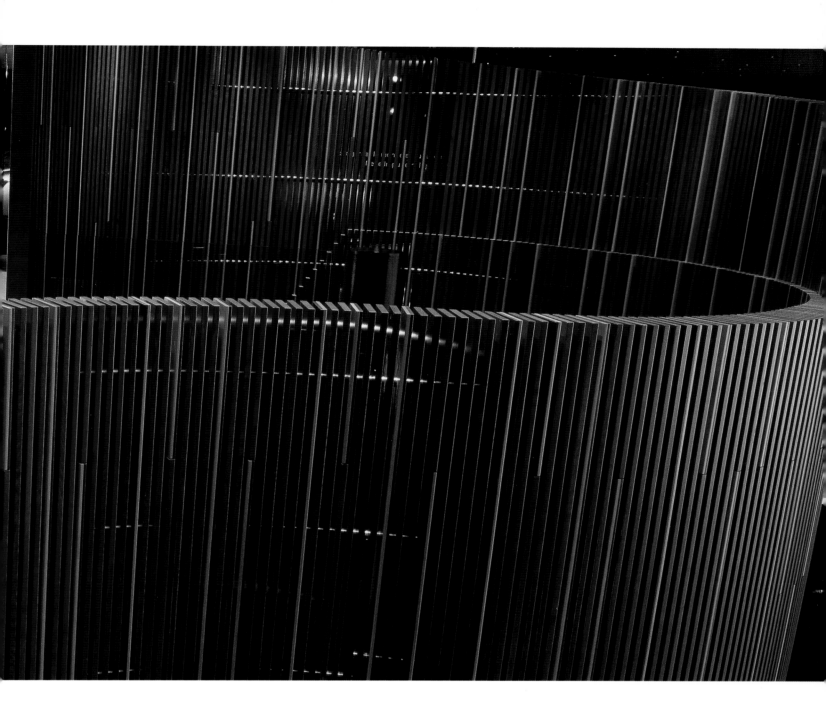

Die räumliche Struktur des Standes bringt neben dem öffentlichen Ausstellungsbereich eine exklusive zweigeschossige Lounge hervor, die Kunden und ernsthaften Kaufinteressenten vorbehalten bleibt. Für die individuelle Beratung und Information stehen hier zwei weitere Fahrzeuge bereit.

The spatial structure of the stand accentuates an exclusive two-storey lounge alongside the public exhibition area, which stays with customers and serious prospective buyers. Two further vehicles are available here for individual consultation and information.

Eine expressiv ge-
schwungene Wendel-
treppe mit Latten-
wangen aus dunklem,
warmtonigem Holz
führt ins Obergeschoss
des internen Lounge-
bereichs.

An eloquently curved
spiral staircase with
slatted wooden side-
walls in a dark warm
tone leads to the
upper-storey of the
internal lounge area.

Ausgewählte, hochwertige Materialien, mit handwerklicher
Präzision und Sorgfalt verarbeitet, und die zeitlose Formensprache verkörpern die Wertewelt der Marke Maybach. Eine
expressiv geschwungene Wendeltreppe aus warmtonigen
Hölzern verbindet die Geschossebenen der Lounge.

Selected, high-quality materials with hand-crafted precision
and care and the timeless form language embody the world of
values for the Maybach brand. An expressive curved spiral
staircase made of warm-tone woods connects the floors of
the lounge.

Im Obergeschoss des internen Lounge-bereichs werden zusätzlich eine zweite und dritte Maybach Limousine präsentiert.

In the upper storey of the internal lounge area an additional second and third Maybach limosine are presented.

Year	**2003**
Location	**Geneva (CH)**
Trade Fair	**International Motor Show**
Exhibitor	**DaimlerChrysler AG, Stuttgart / Maybach**
Complete Organisation	**DaimlerChrysler AG, Dept. MKP/B**
Architect	**Kauffmann Theilig & Partner, Ostfildern-Kemnat**
Lighting	**Design: TLD-Lichttechnik, Wendlingen Realisation: Sound + Light, Leonberg**
Graphics / Communication	**TC Gruppe GmbH, Target Communications, Ludwigsburg**
Size	**about 600 m²**
Realisation	**Ernst F. Ambrosius & Sohn GmbH, Frankfurt a. M.**
Photos	**Andreas Keller, Altdorf**

CULLMANN

variocom
the prime connect

Kabellose Universal-Freisprechanlagen
Cordless Universal Handsfree-Kits

CULLMANN

Schmetterlingssammler
Butterfly Collector

BBF 3D
für Cullmann

BBF 3D
for Cullmann

Verband man den Namen Cullmann früher mit der Entwicklung und Fertigung von Film- und Foto-Stativen, steht er heute für hochwertiges Zubehör im Bereich Car Communication.

Unter einem weißen, textilen Rahmen, der über den Köpfen der Besucher den Stand umfasst und den Firmennamen weithin lesbar macht, stehen auf dem vom Hallenboden nur wenige Zentimeter abgehobenen, dunklen Nussbaumboden zwei Reihen mit Vitrinen. Es sind schmale weiße Körper mit horizontalen Ablage- und Präsentationsflächen aus Holz. Dadurch, dass sie vom Boden abgehoben sind und im Korpus einen Schlitz haben, werden Durchblicke durch den ganzen Stand gewährt.

Previously one may have associated the name Cullmann with the development and production of film and photo tripods, whereas today the name stands for high-quality accessories in the field of car communication.

Beneath a white textile frame, which encloses the stand above head height and ensures that the company name is legible from a great distance, are two rows of display cases standing on the dark walnut floor that is raised a mere few centimetres from the floor of the hall. These cases are narrow white bodies with horizontal wooden storage and presentation surfaces. Since the bodies are raised from the floor and also have slits in them, they afford views of the whole stand.

Grundriss

Plan

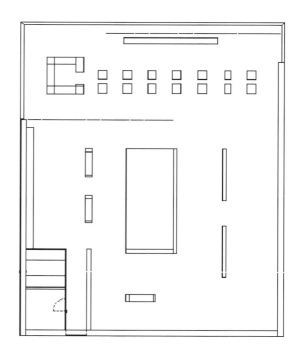

Wie aufgespießte Schmetterlinge in der Sammlung sind die Produkte in hinterleuchteten Fensterschlitzen auf Augenhöhe ausgestellt oder auf schräg gestellten Flächen fixiert.

The products are exhibited at eye level in backlit window apertures like pinned butterflies or are fixed to additional obliquely positioned surfaces.

variocom VC3 voice control .prime dialog

Zusätzlich zu den Features der VC3 dsp

Sprecherunabhängige
Spracherkennung
Ohne aufwendiges Anlernen des
Systems von jedem zu bedienen

voice card mit Telefonbuch

Multilinguale Nutzung
dank einfachem Wechsel

Optimierte Dialogführung

Leicht verständliche Bedienung

Year	**2003**
Location	**Hanover**
Trade Fair	**CeBIT**
Exhibitor	**Cullmann GmbH, Cadolzburg**
Architect	**BBF 3D, Cologne:** **Gero Bruckmann, Robert Tyborski** **designafairs exhibition services GmbH,** **Erlangen**
Size	**130 m² head stand**
Realisation	**Rittmeier und Partner, Cologne** **Furniture: Timmerhues Montagebau,** **Münster**
Graphics / Communication	**Phokus Event Marketing, Nuremberg**
Photos	**BBF Basle (CH)**

... oder mit Kartenlösungen, die im Zahlungsverkehr, im ID-Bereich und in der Telekommunikation jedem Einzelnen persönliche Sicherheit geben.

... to card solutions that guarantee personal security when making payments, providing ID, or using telecommunications systems.

Sei es mit unseren Lösungen im System Banknote, die in über 80 Ländern der Erde zum Einsatz kommen ...

From our banknote solutions, which are used in more than 80 countries around the world,...

The Future of ID Systems

The Future of Payments

Panzerknacker
Safe Breaker

avcommunication GmbH
für Giesecke & Devrient

avcommunication GmbH
for Giesecke & Devrient

Wie ein aufgeschnittener Tresor erscheint dieser aus raum-bildenden, 6,5 m hohen Rahmen mit einer Spannweite von 13 m und Edelstahl-Oberfläche gebildete Messestand. Mit ihrer klaren Formensprache definieren die Rahmen als gestalterische Grundelemente den Raum: aus der Distanz erscheint der Stand geschlossen, mit abnehmender Entfernung wird er transparent, öffnet sich durch die rhythmisch auseinandergezogenen Rahmen, gibt Einblick ins Innere und weckt Neugier. Die Rahmen schützen, halten zusammen und dienen im Innern der hervor-hebenden Präsentation von wertvollen Exponaten, die sie umfangen.

The appearance of this stand, comprising spatially defining, 6.5-metre-high frames with a span of 13 metres and stainless-steel surfaces, resembles a cut-open safe. The frames, as the creative fundamental components, define the area with their clear use of forms. From a distance the stand has a closed appearance; with increasing distance it becomes transparent, opening up through the rhythmically pulled-apart frames to allow a view of the interior and arouse curiosity. The frames protect, keep the whole together and, in the interior, are a vehicle for the presentation of valuable exhibits, which they embrace.

Betritt der Besucher das Standinnere, öffnet sich ihm das gesamte Informationsspektrum. Der zweistöckige Raum gliedert sich in Produkt- und Anwendungsinformationen im Erdgeschoss sowie Besprechungsräume und eine terrassenartige Cafeteria im Obergeschoss.

Der modular aufgebaute Stand, bei dem der Einsatz der Gestaltungselemente strengen Regeln unterliegt – sie gewährleisten die Wiedererkennbarkeit der Marke bei weiteren Messeauftritten –, ist somit nicht nur als Flaggschiff auf der CeBIT geeignet.

Once the visitors have entered the stand's interior, the entire information spectrum is opened up to them. The two-storey area is divided into product and user information on the lower storey and meeting rooms and a terrace-like cafeteria on the upper storey.

The modular-built stand, whose use of design elements is subject to strict rules that guarantee easy recognisability at future trade fair appearances, is thus not only suitable to be the flagship at the CeBIT.

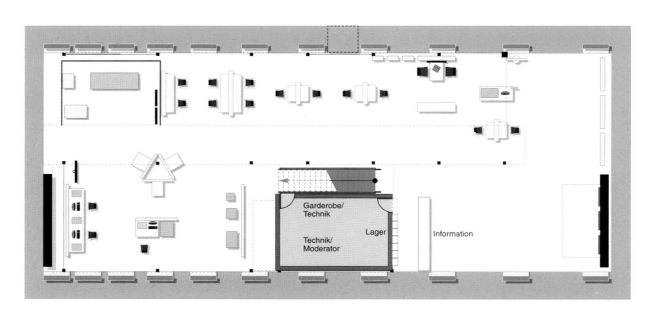

Grundriss

Plan

Garderobe/
Technik

Lager

Information

Technik/
Moderator

Von der Rückseite, an der die Abstände enger sind, wirken die Rahmen wie die Schuppen eines großen Reptils.

From the rear, where the gaps are narrower, the frames resemble the scales of a large reptile.

Year	**2003**
Location	**Hanover**
Trade Fair	**CeBIT**
Exhibitor	**Giesecke & Devrient GmbH, Munich**
Communication Concept / Architecture	**avcommunication GmbH, Ludwigsburg: Adrian von Starck, Andreas Olbrich**
Size	**480 m²**
Realisation	**Zeeh Design Messebau, Puchheim**
Graphics	**Rempen & Partner, Munich**
Photos	**Victor S. Brigola, Stuttgart**

Schlangenlinien
Serpentine Structure

Ludwig Architekten
für Interflex

Ludwig Architekten
for Interflex

Entsprechend dem Motto einer Kampagne für das Unternehmen für Zeiterfassung und Zeitmanagement – „Das Zauberwort heißt Flexibilität" – windet sich eine 40 m lange schlangenartige Theke um zehn leuchtende Informationsstelen. Diese Theke dient der Beratung, der Demonstration von Produkten, Gesprächen und der Bewirtung. Die einzelnen Thekenelemente des modularen Standes haben vier verschiedene Radien und können zu unterschiedlichen Schlangenlinien zusammengesetzt werden. Mobile Unterbauteile für Informationsmaterial und Bewirtung können je nach Bedarf an die Thekenelemente angebaut werden, und ein durchlaufender Kabelschlitz auf der Arbeitsplatte versorgt an jeder Stelle die PCs und Terminals mit Strom.

Corresponding to the motto of a company campaign for time keeping and time management – "The magic word is flexibility" – a 40-metre-long, serpentine counter winds its way around ten bright information steles. This counter is used for consultations, product demonstrations, talks and refreshments. The individual elements of the modular stand have four different radiuses and can be assembled to form variable wavy lines. Mobile base components for information material and refreshments can be attached to the counter element as required, and one continuous cable duct on the work surface supplies the PCs and terminals at all points with electricity.

Die multifunktionale
Theke wirkt mit dem
durchlaufenden
Kabelschlitz wie eine
Carrerabahn.

The multifunctional
counter with its one
long cable duct looks
like a model race track.

Die an den hinterleuchteten Informationsstelen aus Glas ein-
gespannten Grafikdrucke sind austauschbar. Ebenso die
mit Stoff bespannten großen Grafikelemente, die den syste-
matisierten Bürobereich verkleiden.

The graphic prints attached to the backlit glass information
steles are interchangeable, as are the large stretched-fabric
graphic elements that cover the systematised office area.

Year	**2003**
Location	**Hanover**
Trade Fair	**CeBIT**
Exhibitor	**Interflex Datensysteme GmbH & Co. KG**
Architect	**Ludwig Architekten, Köngen:** **Almut Weinecke-Ludwig, Dieter Ludwig**
Lighting	**Raumtechnik Messebau und Event-** **marketing GmbH, Ostfildern**
Size	**360 m²**
Realisation	**Raumtechnik Messebau und Event-** **marketing GmbH, Ostfildern**
Graphics / Communication	**Nic Zoeller, Stuttgart**
Photos	**Andreas Keller, Altdorf**

Blauer Horizont
Blue Horizon

Schmidhuber + Partner / KMS
für O_2

Schmidhuber + Partner / KMS
for O_2

Der Stand, der zum erfolgreichen Launch der Marke O_2 zur CeBIT 2002 entwickelt wurde, zeigt sich in überarbeiteter Form mit konsequenten Weiterentwicklungen und variationsreicherem Kommunikationskonzept. Die äußere Hülle wird gebildet von einer hängenden Konstruktion mit einer luftgefüllten Membran in der CI-Farbe Blau. Schon von Ferne wie ein Horizont erkennbar, trägt sie den Markennamen auf der Außenseite. Der darunter befindliche Präsentationsbereich scheint durch eine Unterleuchtung des Podests ca. 50 cm über dem Boden zu schweben. Auf dieser erhöhten Grundfläche bekommt der Besucher wie in einem Einkaufscenter eine Vorstellung von der Vielfalt des Angebots.

The stand, which was developed for the successful launch of the O_2 brand at CeBIT 2002, is presented in a reworked form with consistent developments and a more variable communication concept. The external skin is formed by a suspended construction with an air-filled membrane in the CI colour blue. Recognisable from afar like a horizon, the brand name is displayed on the outside. The presentation area situated below this appears to be suspended approximately 50 cm above the floor, since the platform is lit from below. On this raised base the visitor is given an idea of the variety of products on offer, as in a shopping centre.

Sechs Lounges im Außenbereich dieser offenen Fläche dienen der vertiefenden Beratung, der Produktdemonstration und -information oder der Entspannung und umgeben eine fast 20 m lange, von beiden Seiten zugängliche Theke mit darüber angebrachten LED-Streifen, auf denen Filmsequenzen zu sehen sind.

Händler, Presse und VIPs werden im OG eines separaten Bereichs im Rückgebäude des Messestandes betreut. Dessen Trennwand besteht aus zehn wassergefüllten, 2,20 m hohen, blau schimmernden Becken, in denen Luftblasen hochsteigen – die dreidimensionale Umsetzung des bekannten Key Visuals von O_2.

Six lounges in the external area of this open space offer an opportunity for detailed consultation, product demonstration and information, or relaxation. They encircle an almost 20-metre-long counter that is accessible from both sides; LED strips showing film sequences are mounted above the counter.

Traders, the press and VIPs are looked after in the upper storey of a separate area in the rear building. The dividing wall comprises ten water-filled, 2.2-metre-high shimmering blue tanks full of air bubbles rising to the surface – the three-dimensional application of O_2's well-known key visual.

Der Besprechungsbereich im Obergeschoss als Lounge mit einer Bar vor blau leuchtender Lichtwand und weißen Sitzelementen auf braunem, langflorigem Teppichboden.

The meeting area in the upper storey takes the form of a lounge with a bar in front of a shining blue light wall and white seating elements on a brown shag-pile carpet.

Year	**2003**
Location	**Hanover**
Trade Fair	**CeBIT**
Exhibitor	**O$_2$ Germany GmbH & Co. OHG**
Concept and Architecture	**Schmidhuber + Partner, Munich: Robert Hagl, Martin Wiedenmann, Susanne Schmidhuber, Julia Schneider**
Concept and Communication	**KMS, Munich: Michael Keller, Wahan Mechitarian, Eva Rohrer, Christoph Rohrer, Birgit Vogel**
Lighting	**Delux: Rolf Derrer, Zurich (CH)**
Size	**1,425 m^2 ground floor 350 m^2 first floor**
Realisation	**Messebau Tünnissen, Kranenburg**
Photos	**Frank Kleinbach, Stuttgart**

Rasenmähen

Mowing the Lawn

mps mediaworks
für PeopleSoft Deutschland

mps mediaworks
for PeopleSoft Deutschland

Auf einer in Stufen ansteigenden weißen Rasenfläche scheinen im kreisrunden Zentrum des Standes vor einer Brand-Wall vier kubische Räume wie Ufos zu schweben. Mit dieser Wiese, die Träume weckt, aber durch die fremde Farbe noch abstrakt genug bleibt, wird ein Ort gezeigt, an dem der Benutzer durch die 100% internetbasierte Software des Unternehmens auch ohne die Infrastruktur des Offices in Real-Time agieren könnte. Info-Panels liegen wie Papier in der Wiese und offerieren die unterschiedlichsten Inhalte.

Hat der Besucher sich im Log-in-Bereich akkreditieren lassen (in Anlehnung an den Zugang ins Internet), darf er den Stand betreten und kann dann sowohl den Portal- als auch den Systembereich kennen lernen. Im Portalbereich lernt er nun mit einer Art Rasenmäher (dem Wower, einem interaktiven Informationstool) spielerisch die Schritte bis zum Real-Time-Enterprise kennen.

On a terraced white lawn, four cubic rooms appear to be hovering like UFOs in front of a brand wall in the stand's perfectly circular centre. This lawn, which awakens dreams yet at the same time retains an abstract quality owing to its strange colour, represents a place in which the visitor could operate in Real Time using the 100% internet-based company software, even without the office infrastructure. Info panels with the most varied contents are strewn on the lawn like pieces of paper.

Once the visitors have gained authorisation in the log-in area (a reference to gaining access to the Internet), they are allowed to enter the stand and acquaint themselves with the portal as well as the systems area. In the portal area they playfully learn the steps leading to the Real-Time Enterprise with a kind of lawnmower (the Wower, an interactive information tool).

Den Systembereich bilden die vier stoffbespannten Kuben, die mit medialer Technik ausgestattet sind und in denen vier unterschiedliche Produkte vorgestellt werden. Im Innern soll der Besucher sich wohl fühlen, deshalb erinnern die Innenräume auch eher an Wohnzimmer als an Besprechungsräume: weißer Filzteppich, kubenförmige, ineinander steckbare Tischchen, bequeme Sessel.

Auf dem weißen Stand sind nur das Logo an der Rückwand und die stark vergrößerten weltweiten Werbekampagnen des niederländischen Illustrators Bas de Gras farbig. Sie bedecken jeweils eine Seite der Kuben und haben einen extrem hohen Wiedererkennungswert.

The four fabric-stretched cubes make up the systems area: these are equipped with media technology and are used to present four different products. Since the visitor is meant to feel at ease, the interior rooms are more reminiscent of a living room than
a conference room: white felt carpeting, small cube-shaped stackable tables, comfortable chairs.

The only colour on the white stand is provided by the logo on the rear wall and the blown-up world-wide advertising campaigns by the Dutch illustrator Bas de Gras. These cover one side of each cube and are eye-catchingly memorable.

Year	2003
Location	Hanover
Trade Fair	CeBIT
Exhibitor	PeopleSoft Deutschland GmbH, Munich
Architect	Design: mps mediaworks GmbH, Munich: Michael Schuster
Communication	the imageneering company (Member of Auratis AG): Andreas Eric Meyer
Size	275 m²
Realisation	Messe Bauer & Companions GmbH, Munich
Photos	PeopleSoft Deutschland GmbH, Munich

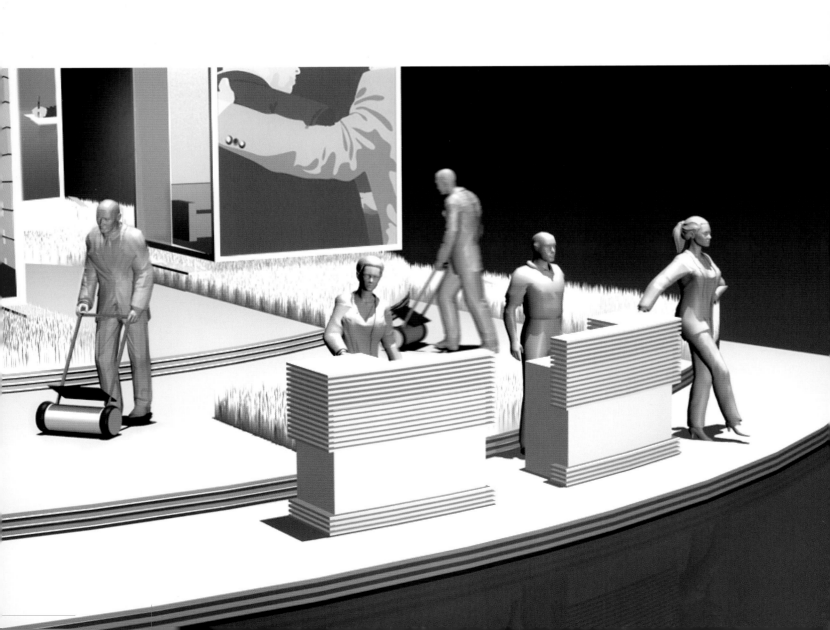

Eingeklammert
Bracketed

HDW Design GmbH
für Tenovis

HDW Design GmbH
for Tenovis

Der im April 2000 an den Start gegangene Dienstleister Tenovis GmbH & Co. KG bietet Business-Kommunikationslösungen rund um das Zusammenwachsen von Telekommunikation und Internet. Als Nachfolgeunternehmen von Telenorma und Bosch Telecom wollte man sich klar abheben und suchte einen auffälligen Messeauftritt. Dadurch, dass der 2-stöckige Teil des Standes in große Spangen eingehängt ist, hat er eine sehr eigene Charakteristik.

Den offenen Bereich dominieren übergroße orangefarbene Klammern, die von weitem in der Halle zu sehen sind. Sie tragen Grafik, bieten ein Rückgrat für die verschiedenen Szenarien für große und mittelständische Unternehmen, für Mobil- und Heimarbeitsplätze und dienen der Abschirmung offener Besprechungsplätze.

The service company Tenovis GmbH & Co KG, which started up in April 2000, offers business-communication solutions in all areas connected with the merging of telecommunications and the Internet. As a successor company of Telenorma and Bosch Telecom, it wished to stand out clearly and sought a conspicuous trade fair appearance. The double-storey part of the stand is suspended using large clasps, giving it a very individual building characteristic.

Extremely large orange brackets, which are visible in the hall from afar, dominate the open area. They are used as a graphics display, provide a backbone for the various scenarios for large and middle-sized companies, for mobile and home work places, and screen off the open meeting areas.

Hinter einer mit Grafik bedruckten, satinierten Glaswand befindet sich ein separater, intimer Bereich für professionelle Anwender.

Behind a satin-frosted glass wall with printed graphics is a separate intimate area for professional users.

Speziell für die
Kundenbedürfnisse
wurden die Möbel
entwickelt. Sie sind
hoch variabel für viele
Ansprüche.

The furniture was
designed specially for
the needs of the clients.
The pieces are highly
variable and meet
many different needs.

Year	**2003**
Location	**Hanover**
Trade Fair	**CeBIT**
Exhibitor	**Tenovis GmbH & Co. KG, Frankfurt a. M.**
Architect	**HDW Design GmbH, Offenbach:** **Udo E. Fischer, Jurek Medrala**
Size	**1,415 m² ground floor** **452 m² first floor**
Realisation	**Bluepool AG, Leinfelden-Echterdingen**
Graphics / Communication	**Atelier Pohlenz, Offenbach**
Show Concept and Realisation	**avcommunication GmbH, Ludwigsburg**
Photos	**Falk Tunnat** **Udo E. Fischer**

Gelbkariert

Yellow Checked

Meiré und Meiré
für Alape

Meiré und Meiré
for Alape

Der Messestand hat die Aufgabe, die Neuausrichtung von Alape zu erklären, die in einer für unterschiedliche Nutzer optimierten Individual-Lösung liegt. Der 4 m hohe, an drei Seiten geschlossene Messestand erhält zusätzliche Ferrnwirkung durch die transparente Wand in CI-Farben.

Der klar strukturierte Innenraum hat keine hohen Wände, wirkt dadurch extrem weit und großzügig und lässt Raum für die Umsetzung des Leitgedankens „shaping space", der bewussten Gestaltung von Räumen. Die Produkte werden durchgängig in Weiß vor grauen Wänden gezeigt. Der Schwerpunkt der Inszenierung liegt somit auf dem Gesamteindruck und nicht wie früher auf dem einzelnen Produkt. Der Besucher wird auf einem Weg geführt, auf dem er dem grundsätzlichen Ablauf des Angebots folgt: von einzelnen Komponenten bis zu Produkten für die Gesamtgestaltung des Badezimmers.

The purpose of the trade fair stand is to announce Alape's reorientation, which lies in an optimised individual solution for different users. The transparent walls of the 4-metre-high trade fair stand in the corporate identity colours increase the long-distance visual effect.

There are no high walls in the clearly structured interior. This gives it an extremely open and spacious feel and allows room for the realisation of the central theme "shaping space", the conscious design of spaces. The products are systematically displayed in white in front of grey walls. In this way, the main focus of the setting is on the overall impression rather than on the individual product, as was previously the case. The visitors are led along a path where they follow the fundamental development of the product range: from individual components to products for the overall design of the bathroom.

Aus einzelnen Elementen bestehende Acrylglas-Abhängungen vor den gelben Wänden sorgen für die außerordentliche Fernwirkung.

Acylic glass hangings in front of the yellow walls, made up of individual elements, give the stand an unusual appearance from a distance.

Im Zentrum des Messestandes gibt es einen Bereich für eine Sonderpräsentation. Daran schließt sich eine große Lounge an, von der aus man den gesamten Stand erleben kann.

In the centre of the trade fair stand is an area reserved for a special presentation. Adjoining this is a large lounge with a view of the entire stand.

Dadurch, dass die Wände im Innern nur halbhoch sind, wirkt der Stand großzügig und offen.

The stand has an open and spacious feel to it as the interior walls are relatively low.

Year	**2003**
Location	**Frankfurt a. M.**
Trade Fair	**ISH**
Exhibitor	**Alape Adolf Lamprecht Betriebs GmbH, Goslar**
Architect	**Meiré und Meiré, Cologne: Dirk Meuleneers Andrea Jürgens, Bad Harzburg**
Lighting	**Alape Interiors-Bereich**
Size	**400 m²**
Realisation	**Alape Interiors-Bereich**
Graphics / Communication	**Meiré und Meiré, Cologne**
Photos	**Alape**

Raum für Produktikonen
Space for Product Icons

Meiré und Meiré
für Dornbracht

Meiré und Meiré
for Dornbracht

Dornbracht hat sich in den letzten Jahren nicht nur mit den zahlreichen Kunst- und Kulturprojekten, sondern auch mit Projekten in den Bereichen Küche, Interior, Licht so weiterentwickelt, dass die Firma zu einem Gestalter von Lebenswelten geworden ist, die auf dem Messestand inszeniert werden.

Die Architektur des modularen Messestandes bietet den Hintergrund, vor dem die Produkte erscheinen. Da die Produkte selbst teilweise zu Ikonen geworden sind, kann die Architektur auf das Zelebrieren verzichten.

Im Zentrum der Grundfläche des Messestandes befindet sich die Inszenierung der MEM-Welt (mem bedeutet auf Esperanto „Selbst"), wo ein Bewusstsein für die immateriellen Werte geschaffen werden soll. Hier kann sich jeder seinen ganz persönlichen Raum für seine individuellen Rituale, seine Stimmungen und seinen Lebensrhythmus aus frei kombinierbaren Armaturen und Modulen zusammenstellen.

Over the past years, Dornbracht has not only developed with the numerous art and culture projects, but also with projects in the kitchen, interior and light domains, turning the company into a creator of living worlds that are produced on the trade fair stand.

The architecture of the modular trade fair stand provides a backdrop for the products. Since some of the products have become icons themselves, the architecture can dispense with celebration.

The new MEM world (mem means "self" in Esperanto) is produced in the middle of the trade fair stand's area, where a concience for immaterial values is to be created. Here anyone can put together their very own personal room for their individual rituals, moods and personal daily rhythm by freely combining fittings and modules.

Wie es in jeder Anzeige
und Broschüre zu
finden ist: Armaturen.
Accessoires. Interiors.
Culture Projects.

Just as is found in any
advert or brochure:
Fittings. Accessories.
Interiors. Culture
Projects.

Ganzheitliche Bad-
architektur für die
Präsentation von
MEM.

Consistent bath archi-
tecture for the presen-
tation of MEM.

Auf einem besonderen
Tisch und in einer
beleuchteten Nische
werden Küchenarma-
turen ausgestellt.

Kitchen fittings are
exhibited on a special
table and in an illu-
minated recess.

Year	**2003**
Location	**Frankfurt a. M.**
Trade Fair	**ISH**
Exhibitor	**Aloys F. Dornbracht GmbH & Co. KG, Iserlohn**
Architect	**Meiré und Meiré, Cologne: Mike Meiré, Dirk Meuleneers**
Lighting	**Winkels Messe- und Ausstellungs-bau GmbH**
Size	**912 m²**
Realisation	**Winkels Messe- und Ausstellungs-bau GmbH**
Graphics / Communication	**Meiré und Meiré, Cologne**
Photos	**Uwe Spöring**

Lichtflügel

Light Wings

Dieter Thiel
für Hansgrohe

Dieter Thiel
for Hansgrohe

Auch diesmal präsentiert Hansgrohe sich mit den Marken Hansgrohe, Axor und Pharo in der Festhalle in einem bühnenartigen Großraum. Ein einfacher Holzboden, eine lichtdurchlässige Decke und segelartige Lichtflügel an den Eingängen bilden einen offenen, hellen Raum für die Präsentation der drei Programm-Marken. In diesem Raumgebilde werden die Produkte in einzelnen, sorgfältig komponierten Szenen in inszenierten Räumen gezeigt, die dem Besucher das Bad als Wohlfühlraum näherbringen.

Once again Hansgrohe makes its presentation with the brands Hansgrohe, Axor and Pharo in a stage-like open space in the festival hall. A simple wooden floor, a light-transmissive ceiling and sail-like illuminated wings flanking the entranceways create a bright, open space for the presentation of the three program brands. The products are shown within this spatial construction in individual carefully composed scenes in stage-set areas, designed to make the visitor more aware of the bathroom as a place of well-being.

Ergänzt wird dieser sehr an der Realisierbarkeit orientierte
Aufbau durch abstrakte lange Wände und Tische mit Zusam-
menstellungen aller Produkte zu einem Thema sowie großen
Foto- und Grafikwänden in unterschiedlichen Ausführungen.

This very realisable construction is complemented by long
abstract walls and tables with all products belonging to a
particular theme grouped together, such as large photo and
graphics walls in various designs.

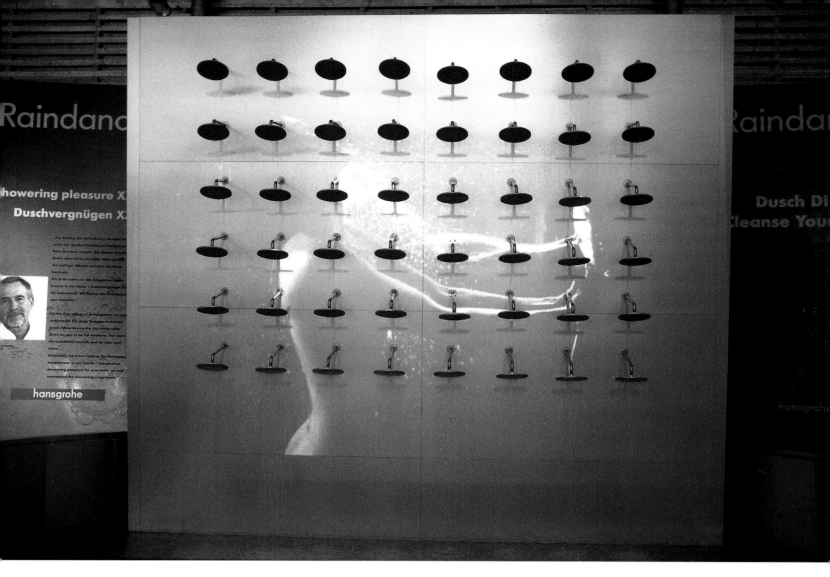

Das neue Produkt „Raindance", das auch den Titel der zur ISH entstandenen Broschüre „bathroom experience 2003" schmückt, ist an einer Wand 48-mal aufgereiht und mit Bildsequenzen überlagert.

The new product "Raindance", which also adorns the title page of the "Bathroom Experience 2003" brochure brought out specially for the ISH, is lined up 48 times on a wall with overlapping image sequences.

Year	**2003**
Location	**Frankfurt a. M.**
Trade Fair	**ISH**
Exhibitor	**Hansgrohe AG, Schiltach**
Architect	**Dieter Thiel, Basle (CH)**
Lighting	**Ansorg GmbH, Mühlheim a.d.R.**
Size	**about 2,000 m²**
Realisation	**Hansgrohe AG Messen und Ausstellungen, Alpirsbach**
Graphics / Communication	**Bangert Verlag, Schopfheim**
Photos	**Klaus Frahm, Hamburg**

Weiß gegen Farbe
White Versus Colour

Laufen AG
Eigenstand

Laufen AG
Own Stand

Erstmals tritt Laufen in Deutschland mit einem eigenen Messestand auf. Der Stand mit seinem überhohen, leuchtenden
Gazekubus und der niedrigeren, dunklen Flanke ist in Schichten
aufgebaut: Zu den Messegängen hin, im stärker frequentierten
Bereich, gibt es eine fast museale Produktpräsentation, be-
gleitet von den Neuheiten in hohen, weißen, transluzenten
Stoffkuben.

Bühnenbildartig inszenierte Räume in dunkelgrauen Kuben
bestimmen „Il Bagno Alessi". Auf einem „roten Teppich"
entlang eines Erlebnisparcours werden dem Besucher die
Produkte beispielsweise in einem Spiegelkabinett oder auch
auf schwarzer Schlacke gezeigt.

For the first time Laufen appeared in Germany with its own
trade fair stand. The stand, with its unusually high, bright gauze
cube and low dark sidewall, is assembled in layers: towards the
entrances to the trade fair, in the more highly frequented area,
is an almost museum-like product presentation accompanied
by the new products in high, white, translucent fabric cubes.

Stage-set areas in dark-grey cubes characterise "Il bagno
Alessi". The products are shown to the visitors on a "red
carpet" running the length of a theme course – in a mirrored
cabinet, for example, or on black scoria.

Die kommunikativen Bereiche mit Catering-zone und Besprechungskuben, die von den beiden Produkt-ausstellungsflächen eingefasst werden, sind farbig und offen.

The communicative areas with catering zone and conference cubes, which are bordered by the two product exhibition areas, are coloured and open.

Dem Besucher wird ein roter Teppich durch die Präsentation der Produkte von „Il bagno Alessi" ausgerollt.

A red carpet is rolled out for the visitor through the presentation of the "Il bagno Alessi" products.

Die Produktpräsenta-
tion vor den Wand-
scheiben innerhalb des
hellen, textilen Kubus
ist streng symetrisch
aufgebaut.

The product presenta-
tion within the bright
textile cube in front of
the wall panels is set up
in a strictly symmetrical
fashion.

Year	**2003**
Location	**Frankfurt a. M.**
Trade Fair	**ISH**
Exhibitor	**Laufen AG, Laufen (CH)**
Architect	**Laufen AG, Laufen (CH): Jürg Heuberger**
Lighting	**Avenion Peter Völker, Hofheim**
Size	**640 m²**
Realisation	**Ernst F. Ambrosius & Sohn GmbH, Frankfurt a. M.** **Ing. Peter Hess, Vienna (A)**
Graphics / Communication	**Laufen AG, Laufen (CH): Jürg Heuberger**
Photos	**Andreas Keller, Altdorf**

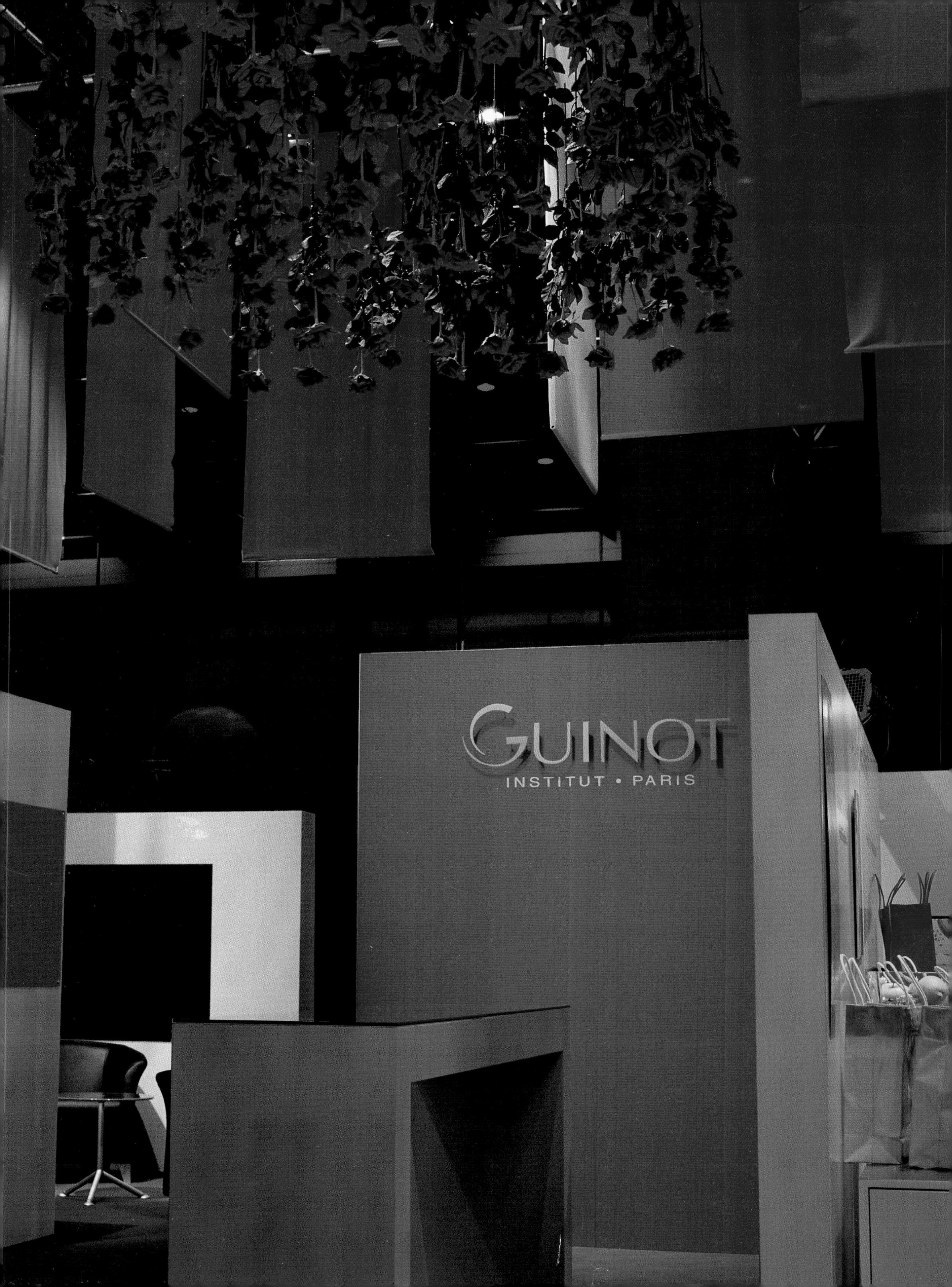
GUINOT
INSTITUT • PARIS